T0196290

How to Date a Stripper...

with **NO** Money Down!

D.P. Sala

authorHOUSE®

AuthorHouse™
1663 Liberty Drive
Bloomington, IN 47403
www.authorhouse.com
Phone: 1-800-839-8640

© *2012 D.P. Sala. All rights reserved.*

*No part of this book may be reproduced, stored in
a retrieval system, or transmitted by any means
without the written permission of the author.*

Published by AuthorHouse 6/26/12

ISBN: 978-1-4772-2519-6 (sc)
ISBN: 978-1-4772-2520-2 (e)

Library of Congress Control Number: 2012911262

*Any people depicted in stock imagery provided by Thinkstock are models,
and such images are being used for illustrative purposes only.
Certain stock imagery © Thinkstock.*

This book is printed on acid-free paper.

*Because of the dynamic nature of the Internet, any web addresses or
links contained in this book may have changed since publication and
may no longer be valid. The views expressed in this work are solely those
of the author and do not necessarily reflect the views of the publisher,
and the publisher hereby disclaims any responsibility for them.*

Introduction

Have you ever wondered how some guys get strippers to go home with them? You have probably noticed that the guys were not much to look at either. You probably think they must have spent a lot of money at the club or used drugs to lure the dancers in. You're probably correct! In this book, I'll teach you how to get with scorching-hot strippers without spending lots of money or using drugs to attract them. You will learn many concepts about the strip club environment and many ways to target the perfect stripper to accomplish your goal of getting a stripper to go home with you. Once you're able to understand how the stripper mentality works and you use some of my proven techniques, you'll be well on your way to having more pleasurable experiences with beautiful exotic dancers! I'm sure a few of my exes and many strip club owners are going to be pissed off when they read this book. Check out *www. stripper-book.com* for updates and seminars that I host in your area.

—Your wingman,
D.P. Sala

About the Author

First of all, thank you for purchasing my book. In addition to this book being very informative, it will also entertain you and your friends and show you the life of a strip club hustler. Before we begin, I just want you to understand my perspective and a little bit more about my background. I graduated from college with a degree in communications and a degree in psychology. After college, I earned a position in pharmaceutical sales. After achieving the number-one rank as a sales representative out of two thousand reps, I moved into a more challenging medical-sales position in a hospital setting. I am currently still a sales rep in the medical and sports field. I have traveled through thirty-eight of the fifty states and have gone to several meetings and sales functions with other sales reps throughout the years. Although most of my time spent in strip clubs was in my mid-twenties, which was also my first couple of years in sales, I still frequent the clubs often and realize more and more about this world of fantasy.

I have learned that from club to club, city to city, stripper to stripper, there are the same basic rules and issues that are constant in this industry. I decided to write this book because guys from all over kept asking me how I knew so much about strippers. They were amazed at how much fun and how much sex I had without spending huge dollars like they did to achieve this. They paid hundreds and received a lot less action from these same girls.

One day, a friend called me and asked how last night at the strip club went. I replied, "I should write a book called *How to Fuck a Stripper with No Money Down!*" He started cracking up, and then I realized I really had something here. I sat down and started brainstorming, writing all the things I knew about strippers and strip clubs. Here we are, a few years later, with my masterpiece in your hand. Now it's your turn to see inside my head and realize that you too can have a much better time at the strip club for a lot less money.

Five Myths about Strippers

- All strippers are in it for the money.

- You have to be good-looking for them to consider going out with you.

- Strippers are held to a different standard than normal women.

- Strippers don't sleep with customers.

- Since strippers are naked most of the time, they like their bodies and don't need compliments.

Contents

I. The Structure of a Strip Club

It is important to understand how the strip club works, because then you can see how you will sometimes get sucked in to paying more money than you need to.

The Cover Charge

Generally, admittance to a club ranges from $7 to $20, depending upon the quality of the club. Additionally, the girls have to pay a tip out each night to work there, meaning they have to give back to the club a percentage of the tips they receive. This additional income to the owner is separate from the cover charges. The dancers will pay an average of a $30 tip out during the week and a $70 tip out on the weekend. If there are twenty girls working a Friday night shift at seventy bucks a girl, the club will receive fourteen hundred dollars right off the bat. That's without even counting the cover charge and booze and additional fees from the "champagne room" that the owner will receive.

Quickly you discover how profitable these strip clubs can be. When you add in a ten-dollar cover charge and multiply that by three hundred guys in attendance, that's three thousand dollars on an average night! That doesn't even include the markup on the liquor and merchandise. The total in just the admittance fees and tip out from the dancers would be about ninety-thousand dollars in just one month. As long as you can tolerate this lifestyle and these beat-up strippers (I mean this in the nicest possible way) and drunk, horny guys every night, you can see how crazy profitable owning a gentlemen's club can be!

The Total Number of Dancers Working per Night

The more dancers working per night, the better things go for the club and for you, the visitor. You may wonder why some clubs have chubby or ugly girls working there. Well, the answer is simply that the club makes money on every girl who works there, so there's no reason to discriminate. Believe it or not, some men prefer bigger girls or even girls with missing teeth. It actually helps some men build their confidence for when the prettier girls come up to them. It's the same as at a regular bar. I like to call them "practice girls." You have to play in a few scrimmage games before you can handle the real deal. You wouldn't want to finally get your chance with a hot chick and blow it early.

It's very hard for a stripper to get fired. As long as they pay tip out and pay the fines for nights they don't show up, they will always have job security. Unless a stripper gets in a fight with the owner or the other girls don't like her and make her feel uncomfortable, she will stay. By the way, that is pretty much the only reason strippers ever quit or leave. I hear from dancers all the time how the girls at the last club were "bitches," and that's why they left the previous club.

Sometimes I'll hear that a stripper told the owner to fuck off, and I can't believe they're still working at that same club. Please understand that these owners know what type of person they're dealing with and have a higher tolerance than most employers. The more money the owner earns from these girls from tip-out and champagne-room fees, the more the owner will tolerate. You won't ever hear of a bouncer telling the owner to fuck off and a week later, he's still working there. They don't produce income for the owner; they only provide safety to the girls, which is easily replaceable.

The number-one reason for strippers leaving their job is that they bounce around a lot in their personal lives. Generally, if they disappear for a while, they'll come back to the same three or four clubs. They only have so many people in their hectic personal lives that they can rely on to help them out—from watching their kids to giving them a ride when their car breaks down. Only a few people will tolerate their inconsistent behavior and emotional instability, especially if they have a few kids or if drug habits are involved. I'll get into that more in the next section.

Exotic Dancers Pay a Tip Out

I mentioned before that dancers pay a nightly fee ranging from thirty to seventy bucks, depending on what night of the week they're working. If twenty girls were scheduled one night, multiply that by sixty dollars per dancer; that equals twelve hundred dollars in profit to the club before they even open the doors. In high-end clubs, tip out can range from $60 to $150 a night. Obviously the weekends are the busiest, and the girls make more, so the club gets a higher rate.

Another thing I found interesting is that the club fines girls for showing up late or calling in sick. A general rule of thumb is if a dancer comes in an hour or two late for her shift, they charge her an additional twenty dollars added on to her tip out. If five girls are late, the club makes an extra hundred bucks in fees that night. If the girl is a no-show, she may get charged an extra 250 bucks.

You may be thinking "Wow!" In actuality, it just causes the girl to work extra hard to pay that off and teaches her that she'd better have a really good reason not to show up for work. Some club owners or "mother hens" (managers) might waive or reduce these fees to the girls. If the owner is fucking the dancer, or if the girl actually has a good reason, the hen might waive the fee, but most clubs do not tolerate this behavior. The club can find a lot of other girls they can count on. Yeah, right! A reliable stripper is an oxymoron!

DJ/Bouncer/Cook—How They Get Paid

The strip club's biggest expense is the DJ, who usually makes four hundred bucks a night or per shift, depending on how long the club is open. Most clubs have two shifts. The opening shift is from 11:00 a.m. until 7:00 p.m. The night shift is from 7:00 p.m. until closing around 2:00 a.m. The DJ makes a flat rate to come in, play all the music, introduce the girls, and announce birthday and bachelor parties. The DJ can average around fifty bucks an hour. You see that can be pretty reasonable. These guys can be your good friends too. They know a lot about these dancers, from their work schedule to what kind of music they like to listen and dance to. What a great intro to a dancer—knowing what kind of music she likes!

These exotic dancers will come in on their days off and practice tricks on the pole to certain songs and get their spins down, especially if they are good pole dancers to begin with or if they see other girls earning big tips from guys; it will motivate them to get better. They'll practice during the slow day shifts, and they usually know that DJ pretty well. There are usually one or two pole specialists the other girls look up to and admire. Generally they are petite and have very strong arms and shoulders. Even though the pole has bearings that help it spin, it still takes a lot of strength and a solid core to spin and rotate upside down on the pole.

Bouncers get paid a separate tip out from the girls and maybe a standard fifty bucks per night from the club. Bouncers are one of the lowest-paid people in the club. At smaller clubs, a maximum of four to six bouncers are usually working per shift. At larger, well-advertised gentlemen's clubs, up to twenty bouncers will be there protecting the fifty to seventy strippers working. There will also be two or three managers—called "coolers"—overseeing the bouncers. Most of the time, the owner is friends with this guy and trusts him at the door or handling the VIP room fees.

Bartenders make an hourly rate and usually get good tips. I'll get into more details about the bartender in the next section.

Finally, there's the cook. Some strip clubs will offer food at lunchtime or just frozen pizzas and small snack foods. Other clubs will have a kitchen serving burgers or an adjoining full restaurant along with the strip club. Most of the time, it depends on what businesses are located nearby. They pay the cook an hourly fee, like most restaurants, and it's not a huge amount of money. It's generally just a convenience for the customer or for the girls to have something to snack on during a shift or after they get off the day shift, which ends at 7:00 p.m. My recommendation is never to eat at a strip club. Do you realize what sits on that counter nightly? Yuck! Unless you're into that kind of stuff.

The Bartender

The bartender is often the most approachable and knowledgeable person in the club. It is very important to find out which bartenders have been there the longest and establish that relationship first. I'll discuss that in more detail in the Strategies section of the book. Usually the most knowledgeable bartenders will work the busy shifts, which can make befriending them a little more difficult. Friday and Saturday nights are generally when they work, but you need to find out if they work day shifts once in a while; then you build your relationship at those times. Those are the best shifts to build your knowledge about the dancers but the worst shifts to practice your skills on the dancers. You'll stand out too much.

Generally, dancers who have had enough of the bullshit of lap dances and are tired of constantly hustling guys eventually move into the position of bartender. It's an easy transition, because they know the club and the dancers. They also already know a bunch of the regulars in the club, after dancing for them previously. An average bartender can knock down five hundred dollars a night behind the bar. Most dancers only make two to three hundred bucks on an average night at a decent strip club. We're not talking about strippers in Vegas. Those girls average much much more. I'm talking about your run-of-the-mill, average truck-stop strip club or the gentlemen's club out in no-man's land. I'll discuss later in the book how underage dancers earn drink tickets from the bartender and how this affects your wallet.

Tip Walks

There are basically two types of tip walks. The first kind happens when the stripper does a dance and then comes off the stage and takes a lap around the club, asking you if you'd like to tip for her show. That dancer may skip that front row as she exits because she has already milked you out of your money when she was on stage. The second type of tip walk happens when all the girls are called onto the stage by the DJ, and they offer a special, like three-for-one dances, which are a bargain. Sometimes the club will offer free T-shirts or a hat with the dances, so you have something to go home with! (This is a terrible idea if you're married, so you'll see guys leave these free goods behind a lot.)

At this point, to avoid getting sucked into this financial trap, refrain from any eye contact whatsoever. Get up and hit the bathroom; go outside and smoke—whatever it takes to avoid that costly mess. While coming up to you after their stage dance on the tip walk, some dancers will ask you if you'd like a lap dance after they're done. For every lap dance she gets lined up, she can shorten that tip walk. The hungry dancers will continue that walk for every dollar, though. Watch out for them.

Another fee the dancer won't inform you about if you do get sucked into a lap dance in the back room is the VIP room surcharge. The "champagne rooms" vary from club to club in what actually can go on in there, and the fees can get pretty costly. Be sure to ask what is included in the fee. Sometimes champagne is included, hence the name. Other times, you are paying for the privacy and the freedom to touch or be touched by the stripper. The VIP area is usually roped off and somewhat visible to others. It has a per-hour fee to go in there that the club gets and a certain rate the stripper gets, which she will split with the house. For example, one hundred bucks an hour for the VIP area and two hundred bucks for the girl will buy you sixty minutes with her. The club will keep the hundred-dollar fee and take a portion of the two hundred dollars to pay the bouncer who watches the activities in that area.

The champagne room activities are a little different. It's usually more secluded, and a lot more physical contact can happen in there, even in strip clubs that enforce the "no contact" rule. They seem to never apply in this area. The girls know for that premium price, they better keep you happy and entertained. They know how to read you, and they know what they are willing to do with you for a certain price. Exotic dancers also know what other girls will do for you, and if you can go to another girl for a better time, they'd better step up their willingness.

Since the owner is getting a percentage and the dancer a portion, they allow more to go on for that premium price. I've mentioned the myth that all strippers are in it for the money. It's a myth because most dancers seem to draw the line somewhere, depending upon the customer. If they just wanted money, they would fuck every customer. They seem to walk that fine moral line between teasing and pleasing each customer on an individual basis.

Small-Town Clubs versus Big-City Clubs

There are differences in clubs and rules that I have noticed throughout the years. I have found that the girls in small-town clubs seem to have lower expectations and come from less, so they are willing to do more for less money. Thirty bucks goes a long way in these clubs. It's like shopping for clothes at Wal-Mart. They might fit a little wrong and not last as long, but you'll get your money's worth and a whole new wardrobe for thirty bucks! Bigger cities have more girls working per night and more turnover, so it's harder to build a relationship with these exotics. Plus, your competition at these small-town clubs is minimal. These strippers get the just-passing-through truck driver killing time or the local farm guy who's stopping in because his wife is out of town. They also get the occasional bachelor party crowd coming through because they wanted to get out of town, since their future wife would not approve of their behavior. These places are gold mines for you to have your pick of the girls. You might have to drive out of the way a bit and put in more time with these girls, but the payoff is well worth the investment. I'll dive deeper into this in the testimonials section.

Full Nudity versus Full Contact

The location of strip club and the county they are located in usually determines if a strip club can be full or partial nudity or a bikini-type strip club. If they serve liquor and have a liquor license, usually the girls have to wear bikinis. Full nudity is usually allowed at establishments where you bring your own booze and they store it in a cooler. You also might find clubs that serve liquor offer full nudity, but only behind the scenes in the roped-off rooms. If a club doesn't have a liquor license, they usually charge higher covers to get in. Additionally, higher tip outs are paid by the strippers to offset the loss in profits made by an absence of liquor sales. Stay away from these clubs, because these girls are trained to make their money on dances. Full contact happens mostly at clubs where the girls wear bikinis. If they're going to let you rub or grab them, usually they want some barrier between your hands and them, even if it's just a tiny thong up their ass.

In my experience, if the dancer is digging you, no matter what type of club you're at, if you ask them and move at their pace, they will let you do anything—within reason. It's just like high school. Start feeling them up their shirt, and if they don't resist, then move south. It's no different here. Go through the bases. First base, second base, and so on. Many clubs will be a combination of these types—no touching in the main room, but the girls might get completely nude. Then, if you want to pay a higher price for the lap dances, they will move you to a roped-off, more secluded area. Then you will be able to touch. If you go even deeper, to a curtained room or champagne room, you can do even more. Trained strippers will know how to tease and tempt you more and more by getting you drunk. Smart clubs might offer free shots in these roped-off areas because they know your judgment will become impaired. At the end of the night, by getting you drunk, it has resulted in milking more money out of you. It's brilliant!

Bringing in Headliners to Boost Attendance

Every couple of months, certain clubs will bring in a headliner, an ex-porn star or a traveling Penthouse model. The club will pay them five to seven thousand dollars for a three-night show. The owner will also pay for a hotel and all expenses. That exotic dancer made her money before you ever walked in the door, which is good for you. However, she is there to work the pole and stir up business so that the other girls get more dances. This way, the club makes more money. Boosting attendance is her main reason for being there if the owner marketed her properly. She is *not* there to be locked down by you. For the most part, don't waste your time or energy on her. She is just passing through.

One angle you actually could use her for is to tell the strippers that you're really interested, in that you'd rather spend time getting to know *them*. You're not interested in some washed-up, D-list celebrity passing through. This *could* backfire on you if your stripper admires the visiting talent, but that is highly unlikely. Let the other suckers in the club waste their time on that main attraction. The other strippers there will probably be glad when she's gone, because they will want the attention back on them. Exotic dancers are all attention-whores!

When you're in there, tell the stripper that you are interested; tell her you would rather spend time with her, and show no interest in the headliner. This will go a long way for you.

Buying a VIP Membership for Entry and Friends

One of the best investments I ever made was buying a silver VIP membership for my friend and me. We went to this club six times, and it had a seven-dollar cover charge. The silver VIP allowed me free entry for a year and only cost me a hundred bucks. I bought myself and my college friend one for two hundred bucks total. We went three times a week for six months. Do the math! We saved a ton of money. The membership also included thirty minutes in the roped-off VIP area and free entry for two of my friends. We still had to tip the girls, but the private area didn't cost us a dime. I'll explain this in more detail in the Testimonials section.

Using the Bartenders and Bouncers for the Breakdown of the Strippers

These employees are the hidden treasures at any strip club. The bartenders are the best; they are generally women who have been there the longest. They don't have the zip they used to have, but they know the customers and the dancers very well. Many bartenders have been roommates with some of the girls passing through. Use them as a source to find out what types of strippers you are dealing with. The next chapter will explain why it is so important to understand what type of dancer they are. Then we will know who to target first.

Mother Hen

This is just a fancy name for the manager of the dancers. The hen controls the girls' schedules and sometimes collecting the tip out. Mostly she is there to deal with all their bullshit, from stealing customers to stealing boyfriends. I've seen this position become less and less needed or wanted these days. Now the general manager has this role in the club. Sometimes the men just don't want to deal with all the strippers' bullshit and will hire a woman to run them. If the hen does exist, she is likely the gossip queen. She will know and thrive on telling you anything you need to know about the dancers—if they have multiple boyfriends, likes, dislikes, turnoffs, you name it.

Most of the time, the hen will have her favorite girls, and she will show some jealousy toward others. Chances are, the hen used to dance ten years ago at this club and really doesn't have the option to leave, so the owner created this position of manager to keep a hold of the business. Managers generally trust this person, and she's the eyes and ears in the club. The problem with any cash business is that if you're not personally there, everybody will steal from you.

The Champagne Room

Different strip clubs are structured slightly differently, but overall they all have a designated area for private dances. Recently, I was in a higher-end club in Florida. The girl asked if I needed anything. I threw out that a blow job would be nice. She then proceeded to figure out a way to make that happen for me, for the right price, of course. She was new to the club and didn't want to get busted, but she proceeded to tell me that in the roped-off area, there are rooms with curtains. We could go back there for an hourly fee, and if I bought champagne, they would close the curtain so the bouncers couldn't see in. Then she said we could do whatever I wanted in there. It was too pricey for me, starting at three hundred dollars plus the price of the champagne. But I liked this girl's ambition. I asked her what her split with the house was, and I told her my friends would pay more outside the club if she could learn to trust me. We became friends, and I hook my friends up with her all the time when she needs extra cash. Now I get my dances from her for free. Win-win, baby!

Other strip clubs will have couches set up, and exotics will bring their regulars back there. It's usually behind closed doors, with a bouncer outside for safety reasons. Pretty much whatever the girl negotiates can happen in there. Over time, the bouncers develop a sense of how willing each girl is, so they know if a guy is crossing the line or not. That's why these bouncers are so valuable, because of the information they have on strippers. The problem is, you may never see these guys, because they might always be in the back area.

I had one girlfriend who liked to go back to the champagne room with me. We would take different strippers into the champagne room from time to time. We would just pay the lap-dance fee, and the dancer would tell the bouncer, "These guys are my regulars." One stripper used to finger my girl and make out with her and pull my cock out, and they would take turns sucking it. It was a crazy, wild time that I never knew could even happen in there. It goes on more than you think. It was then I realized that the rules are meant to be broken.

Once in a while, I would see cake back there, for a stripper's birthday or the club's anniversary. They would feed us cake while dancing and goofing around. It just depended on how well you knew them and if they trusted you or not. Telling the girls your occupation is huge. Obviously, cops are frowned upon. Stating that you're a business owner of any kind is good.

Monopoly Money

Different clubs use different names for their fake cash. From cheetah bucks to kahoots cash, it's all the same. Basically, this is the club's way to accept credit cards and give you fake club money, like Monopoly money, to spend only at that club. I've had several rich friends bring me in to learn how to enjoy their strip-club experience more. One guy went in and ran his credit card for two thousand dollars. Our group of four guys received five hundred each in cheetah bucks. You can only imagine how much fun you can have for five hundred dollars, when you're used to only spending fifty bucks or less. The best part is, I had to spend it. I couldn't pocket it like cash and spend it elsewhere. I was forced to invest it wisely. That was the important thing I did in that situation.

One option could've been to blow that five hundred on some hot dancer, to hang out for a few hours and probably have a great time just for that night. My second option could've been to spread it around to several dancers, getting a taste of them all, so to speak. I barely would have been remembered that way. The best option, and what I chose to do, was decide what would make a lasting impression. I decided to pick out the key people in the club to spend it on. I tipped the floor man fifty bucks to tell me who was worth my time. I then tipped a hundred each to three dancers who knew that club inside in out and would remember me in the future. Then another 150 dollars I spent randomly on the bartender and the shot girl.

The key for me was to invest that money wisely, so the other three guys would enjoy the fifteen hundred bucks they were going to spend. The guy who fronted all the money said he had the best time he has ever had, spending less than the five thousand he usually blows. He still calls me regularly when he's in town to take him out, because he always knows I'm going to increase his knowledge and the good time he has in the gentlemen's club. From time to time, he will even hire me when he has clients in from Japan, to come along and teach these guys what to say. It's a learning experience for them to take home, as well as the visual pleasure these guys get from the girls. He nicknamed me "the stripper Hitch!" after the Will Smith movie.

Another reason to give fake cash that is run off of a credit card is the owner is less likely to get ripped off. If the girls lose or don't turn in that fake money, the owner already got paid and makes more cash this way. I talked earlier about the owners getting ripped off in a cash business; this helps eliminate that. The owner's only concern is that the fake money should not be able to be duplicated very easily. As with casino chips, coins are good to use, with the logo on them or something that is made only for that strip club. The owner's signature could be embedded on it. Something like that would work nicely.

II. The Six Classifications of a Stripper

The Rookie

It is her first couple days on the job. She doesn't know what to expect, and more importantly, she does not have her sales routine down. This is your best chance to score, because she doesn't have a predetermined mindset on how guys are yet. She is very nervous and wants to fit in and will allow more with your advances. The rookie will stay away from dancers who are lifers or businesswomen. Some of the other types of strippers have already cornered her and succeeded in scaring her into not asking men for dances.

Usually this will happen to the cute new girl who just started. The businesswomen want her out. There is only so much money to go around on any given night. The fewer dancers at the club per night, the more money each dancer can make. This is the mindset of the business-type stripper. These girls are very strong and territorial with their regulars. The rookie is different. She probably started off at Hooters and is stepping up her game to the next level. I estimate about seventy percent of these newbies won't last a week. If they don't make good money or feel comfortable doing this, they won't stick out the humiliation long enough to become desensitized to the nature of the strip club.

I love approaching these girls the best, because they aren't guarded and don't have any expectations of what is going to happen in there. You actually get to lead the encounter. You have the edge in these situations and can use this to your advantage. Plus, you can steer her in the right direction and be her friend, filling her in on the "crazy strippers" she should avoid. Remember, you are collecting as much information on every girl in that place as possible. You need to be an undercover detective. The key is to stay off the radar.

Don't say too much; just read the situation and play helpful, not sneaky. This girl will make the rounds and come back to you, often with a huge grin on her face. She will see what you planted in her head and start the conversation with you, agreeing that you're right about certain strippers. This technique is beautiful. It's like she sees that you're right and will instantly trust you, which will last far into the future.

This type of stripper is my favorite. She's green, and who better than you to persuade and manipulate her! Trust me, after a few months, she will be the one manipulating men, so catch her early. Be that first guy she made the mistake with and gave her number to and slept with.

The College Student

This type of dancer is my second-favorite type. They tend to be a little shy at first. They generally work out of town, rather than in the city they grew up in and usually not the town that their college is in. They need to make money to pay for tuition and support their loser boyfriend, in most cases. They are generally younger in age and do not have children. This type of dancer is very fun and outgoing and will go to strip clubs to unwind on her day off. She is often ashamed of stripping and will not discuss her job at school or with friends.

She is not overly concerned with how much money she makes a night, as long as she can cover her tip out and her other college expenses. If this dancer stays in the profession long term, she will eventually become the business-type dancer and do it for the money. You have a short window to catch her early, before she gets use to the easy money and lifestyle. Once she gets out in the real world and works hard for fifty thousand dollars a year, she could resort back to this lifestyle. Only a small percentage of the dancers (around 10 to 15 percent) ever do this, but it can happen. Even a smaller amount of dancers ever graduate college. Their commitment level to anything is usually minimal, as I'll mention in several sections.

If you're talking to a dancer in her early thirties with a college degree, is it very likely that she danced in college years ago. You should avoid this girl, because obviously she came back for the money. It's unlikely she enjoys grinding on bald, fat guys until two in the morning when she could have a respectable day job. There are exceptions to every rule, so you might find the unicorn in every group, but as a rule, this girl is looking for someone to take care of her after her initial "young" phase of dancing. So remember to catch her early in the process.

The Prostitute

This stripper is absolutely the most dangerous. She is generally a little older, around thirty. She has tried leaving the lifestyle but can't leave the money or is afraid of her pimp. She figures she might as well maximize her income potential, since her morals are as low as they come. Usually she has kids or a drug habit to support. Sometimes she will have a pimp at the strip club at the end of the bar who negotiates the terms and the hotel with you, so the dancer doesn't draw attention, since it's against the law in most states.

This girl will approach you and have the most confidence of the dancers. She will start off slowly and ask you for lap dance and test you. She will rub the inside of your thigh and work her way up, offering a little more pleasure each time. Then, if you react to her advances and she finds out you're not a cop, she will go in for the kill. You need to avoid this stripper like HIV. Think about it—it's hard to avoid a girl who grabs your cock or kisses you on the cheek right off the bat. She will be very forward and cut to the chase the fastest once she trusts you. Her goal is to find out if you want a dance and then how far you want to go and what kind of money you're willing to spend. There are no rules with this girl. Anything goes, which is awesome but *costly*.

Generally this girl works in packs and is very territorial. Her pimp will usually have three or four girls in that club. He's in with the owner, and if you become a regular, they will want to know your occupation. When a new girl starts, they will encourage her to join their group, to make even more money, but once that girl denies their proposition, they will keep her separate. They are a close-knit group. I never cared much for these groups and always kept my distance, once I found out the game they play. At some clubs, they will be called the Russians or some particular nationality, because they stay with their own kind.

The Junkie

This particular exotic works so she can make the connections and have the money to support her drug habit. She might have a kid but generally is selfish and just wants to party. This woman comes in all ages. The older ones are easier to spot, from the dark circles under their eyes (don't mistake those circles for just being plain tired) to the possible track marks on their arms. It takes a long time and lots of drug abuse to develop these symptoms. These types of strippers will hang in a tight group and don't venture out unless they need a fix and they trust you. They are afraid of getting caught and will offer free services to get out of a tough jam if needed.

The strip club, to this girl, is just the warm-up part of her night. She will usually party before and during club hours and late night within a small group. She is not interested in sex unless she can get free drugs out of the deal. Sex is the outcome of coming off the high or passing out. Very dirty exotics go to after-parties. Think about it—they go there knowing the guys want sex, and they are willing to give it up for feeling good for a few hours. It's just a barter of services, which is sad when you think about it.

How is this different than taking a woman to dinner and feeding her and then trying to get fed? In my experience with this category of strippers, they seem to be the most experienced in the bedroom. They have this kinky side to them and are very open to trying new things. Possibly, it is the drug ecstasy that moved them forward or the men wanting sexual fantasies and favors for the drugs, so these girls tend to do more threesomes and S&M. These girls just want to feel accepted and generally do drugs in groups or with a girlfriend who shares the same habits. Naturally these girls are into three-ways and toys to go along with their drug fix . Think about how expensive their drug habit can get. It adds up very fast. Not only are you paying for one bad habit; now double it with her friend. Drug users in general hate to do drugs alone. It's like dating a girl with a kid. You take them out to eat, and the bill comes for three instead of two. Ouch!

If you're into drugs yourself, you have an instant "in" with these girls, so you might want to target these types. Personally, I'm a non-drug user, so my strategies focus on picking up dancers without using drugs to lure them in. I have one friend who smokes weed, and his line at the end of the night was always, "Would you like to smoke back at my place after work?" Nine out of ten times, if they thought he was nice and had a decent conversation, they would join him. They would ask if they could bring a friend, and *Shazam*, he was in like Flynn! He's told me some great stories of experiences he's had, but I'll let him write his own autobiography someday.

The Lifer

This dancer has been doing it for twenty years. She most likely has children and has had multiple surgeries to look that good. She tends to be in her late thirties and works out a lot. This type of exotic dancer doesn't know any other profession. She has tons of regulars who see her weekly. It's hard for you to get in her rotation unless you are willing to spend lots of money. This girl has a guy who pays her mortgage, a different guy who pays her car payment, another guy who pays her cell phone bill. You get the idea. The more they pay, the more time she spends in and outside of the club with them. She only works a few months at a time and will pop up at a club when she needs new victims to pay her bills. As one guy drops off her roster, she will need to add a new sucker. I'll tell you more on this type of stripper in the Confessions section of this book. When you get on her disabled list (i.e., stop paying her bills), she has to go out and recruit new players.

This girl is probably the most intelligent and best conversationalist of the types, along with the businesswoman. She can usually hold the interest of these successful businessmen with her body and her mind, which is actually very hard for a stripper to do. But you'd better be willing to cough up the Benjamins if you want to stay on her list of to-dos. This woman is always searching for love. They are so fucked up in the head, they think guys will actually trust and respect them. After twenty years of working in this business, they think the strip club fantasy mentality is real life. They are usually on antidepressants or anxiety pills.

Another thing to know is that these types of strippers especially like the flexible work hours. If they have their kids part or most of the time, they can make in two shifts what most jobs pay in a forty-hour work week. This is another reason for you not to pursue this type. They need the money even more than the businesswoman, in most cases.

These dancers tend to have done it all. They are very experienced with other women. They have had multiple men at a time. They usually have tried it all, since their moral value is at a super low, having done this job for so long.

The Businesswoman (aka: the Grinders)

This stripper is the most dangerous to your bank account. She will lead you on, but it's all about the money. She can easily average $1500 a night and saves most of it or supports her big house and lifestyle with this income. She is very independent. If she decides to have sex with you, it's simply a business transaction to her; not like the prostitute who has quotas. It's because she likes you, and it's partially like an escort job to her. It's different from a prostitute, where no standards are involved. Stay away from these girls, because they are trained not to give you sex, because then you'll move on and not tip them anymore. They are practically trained to tease and manipulate you to the fullest.

The few girls I know in this category are constantly improving their looks. These dancers get Botox injections, multiple boob jobs, a nose job, veneers, etc. They are very pretty and competitive because like in sales, they want to stay on top. Their ego is involved too. It's like a cash hold 'em player. The best players play without pride. They might play only five premium hands all night in four hours but will win a thousand bucks. These dancers might only have four customers come in and make three to four hundred on each customer. That beats hustling forty guys for three dollars each and getting six or seven lap dances and making two hundred bucks all night. Both are decent shifts, but the standard is different for the different types of strippers.

I tend to get the most challenged mentally by these girls. I love the way they think. I would hire these girls in a heartbeat to be salespeople. They have mastered this world and are to me the second most dangerous type of stripper. They don't have pimps, so the prostitutes to me are the most dangerous. These girls are smart enough not to have to pay a cut to the pimp. They filter and pick their victims (us men) at a high level. Oh, and by the way, this girl is the hardest to spend any time with, unless you are paying for it.

III. The Mind of a Stripper

The Stripper Paradox

A stripper is completely delusional. She usually sees things one way, and she will convince herself she is not like the other girls. But in all actuality, she is exactly what you think she is. Her self-perception is all messed up. This concept is one my friend and I noticed. Basically, we were picking on one stripper for being a whore and a gold-digger and that she had a price that she would do anything for. She said, "I'm not that way. I don't see guys as dollar signs. I'm not a whore and don't sleep around." The list went on and on.

I don't know why she was in denial, because once we busted her out on how many guys she was fucking and how we knew that she lived in a motel (a weekly motel that a married guy paid for and banged her at), she freaked out. All of this information I had gathered from the bartender and bouncers, who warned me not to get sucked in. She felt stupid and still tried to deny that this was what was really going on. She was trying to justify and rationalize her antics. It was ridiculous.

I call it the stripper paradox because they have two conflicting lives that they somehow blend into one and feel what they are doing is right. By the way, busting a stripper out is never good for your reputation in the strip club. It's not like the other girls were mad at me, but after she told them I knew all this stuff about her, I lost their trust and hers. Strippers never want to be held accountable for anything. So be careful of what you tell a stripper you know about her. Keep the details out, and stay positive with what you know. Tell her how sweet she is and that she is a good mom or is well-liked in there, even if it's all bullshit. Absolutely do not bust her out. It will only hurt you. It's like when you're young and your parents teach you, "If you don't have anything nice to say, don't say anything!" This applies here. I wish I would have learned that!

High-Maintenance Dancers vs. Survival-Mode Strippers

Depending upon what phase or type or combination of stripper you're dealing with, her mentality changes. Most small to midsize towns where dancers work have girls who are struggling financially. These exotics are in survival mode most of the time. They have the ability to make obscene amounts of money each week but then don't show up to work for two weeks. That's where their lazy, inconsistent side kicks in. They get rich and then don't continue to make the money to get ahead. They will blow it on shopping or paying their cell phone bills or late car payments. They seem, from my experience, to only work when they need the money for something—speeding tickets, DUIs, or some bill that they are behind on. They are always playing catch-up on their bills.

The larger-town girls have better clientele, more bills, and a higher lifestyle in general.

They tend to be more competitive and hustle better for your money. I have had better luck with the smaller-town clubs and midsize-town clubs in general. The quality of stripper tends to be less desirable at these clubs, but then again, *quality stripper* is an oxymoron too. If you do find a scorching-hot stripper at these small-town clubs, she tends to be the one all the guys want anyway, so good luck getting her time for free. Plus she probably has a boyfriend, so lower your standards and move on.

Their View of Men

From trust issues to absentee parents to age, none of it matters to them. Let's address their trust issues first. By working in the club, they see all types of men—married men, engaged men, you name it. Since these strippers see and deal with all types of dishonest men, they sometimes develop a wall or barrier toward all men. The strippers generally don't trust any man. It makes sense; if I met all types of women and they let me fondle them or worse, I would begin to believe that most women would react this way. It's sad but true. Here's the other side to that: Most of these girls are in relationships of some sort and justify what they do because it's their job. In return, they don't trust themselves, so how could they ever trust you?

Secondly, let's look at their absentee parents. Realize that most of these girls have had an absentee father or mother to not help guide them through life. That's why the first boy who gave them any attention at fourteen years old probably knocked them up. Being an older guy (forty-five to fifty-five years of age) can work to your advantage. They will put trust in you and not feel as threatened when you make your move. The younger boys try to pick them up and act all cocky, and in most cases, if the girl is younger, she is not used to the less cocky way you approach her. Have you ever seen a twenty-one-year-old boy hit on a girl at a bar? It's awful. Some strippers actually prefer older men, not because you have money, but because there are no strings attached. You have to play the angle that you are more experienced sexually and can bring out more of their desires and can fulfill their needs better than the two-pump chump can. Plus there is no threat of them falling in love. Isn't that exactly what we are trying to accomplish? Get in and out!

There's more on this in the Strategies and Approaches section of the book.

The bottom line is that your age doesn't matter. Not being gross matters! As long as you are clean-cut and smell nice, you have a chance, from age twenty-five to seventy-five. Most dancers don't really care about your age. In fact, they might think if you're older, you'll spend more money on them outside the club, and in return, this works to your advantage.

Deadbeat Dad or Creepy Uncle Drove Them to This

Their view can be altered because they were molested or raped as a child by a boyfriend or relative. They could have a very low self-worth and self-image. These damaged strippers use the strip club as outlet to fit in or get revenge on men. It's important to understand that some of these girls will turn out okay and some will not. It's almost impossible to tell if they are telling you the truth; if they do open up, generally you can assume they really must trust you. However, what you need to realize is that some of these dancers who were raped or molested will use the strip club as a way to tease men and manipulate you like they were manipulated. You need to stay away from these girls. An easy way to find out is to ask if they have ever dated a guy from the club. If they say no, don't try to be the first. Move on, because you're spinning your wheels with this girl.

Other girls who have recovered will just have a low self-worth or self-image, and that's what you need to go for. It might seem bad, like you're taking advantage of them from an early childhood issue, but aren't we all products of our childhood? I'm just saying that these girls are willing to do more sexually because they don't have that emotional bond or attachment to sex. They seem a little cold, but that's okay. We're not trying to marry them.

Strippers Are Competitive

This always works to your advantage. Strippers want what other girls have. One point to make here before we dig deeper into this in the Strategies section and the testimonial experience I had is that the competitiveness they have is much more than just their boyfriends and their outfits; it's also their lifestyle.

Banging the Boss

At all times, the owner has at least one of the girls on his roster. Special gifts and treatment are given to these girls, and they make him money. There is no jealousy involved here. It is strictly money- and business-driven. Emotions are not involved in this one, from the owner's perspective. He will be loyal to his wife in this matter. Strictly sex and the insight into other strippers is what the owner needs and wants from this dancer. He wants to know who's ripping him off or skimming. These girls are like undercover moles in his operation. Don't get me wrong; you don't want to piss her off, and since you are not spending big bucks in his club, you'll want to be nice to her, but in my experience, don't chase this girl. You want to keep your distance from her and not let her know what you're up to. Appear as if you're just the lonely guy who likes to feel accepted. Pity is never a bad thing in a strip club.

Strippers also like shopping sprees, and owners like taking them on shopping sprees.

When the owner buys them gifts, it makes him feel as if he's on top of the world. He can throw around a lot of cash to boost his ego. It gives him that edge when more new girls start that he can boost them up to the next level. Obviously good owners will help the girls learn how to increase liquor sales and teach them how to give more lap dances.

One of the best owners of a strip club that I became friends with made his money in a pyramid-type sales job, selling supplements for the body. He got involved in the early '80s, and by 1990, he made a million plus. He purchased his first strip club in 1991 for a million cash. He was only in his mid-thirties at this point. He then proceeded to remodel and re-invent this club. He positioned the stages differently and added a shower out in the middle of the main area for the girls to wash each other (which was genius), and really just fine-tuned the girls to be more aggressive and make money. By the late 1990s, that place was a gold mine. He was married and had three kids and was family man by day. At night, he was a hustler. He pretty much had one manager and one girlfriend at the club who kept an eye on everything, but every night before closing, he would stop in to count the money. He knew the average dollars that the club would generate each night, and as long as the money was close to that amount, he was cool with it.

One experience I had that I will never forget involved him. On Wednesday nights, if the strip club was slow, he would grab his limo driver and a handful of hot strippers and take them to my town, where we had a fun dance club that was jumping on that night. The dance club in my town had hot body contest for girls and guys and cheap drinks. He would show up with four or five strippers dressed in skimpy clothes and take them out dancing and drinking all night. As I used to go into his club mainly on Thursday and Saturday nights, we became friends, and he would buy me a drink, and so on. So naturally, when I saw him here, forty-five minutes away from his club, I would say hi or buy him a drink but stay low key.

Obviously he didn't mind the attention, walking in with four hot, half-naked exotics, but still he respected me for keeping him on the down low. Sometimes I would ask the girls who were with him to dance, but I always made sure it wasn't his main girl. Once we became better friends, he invited me to join them for breakfast after the dance club closed. I jumped in the back of the limo, feeling like a rock star, and we proceeded to go to the local Denny's. His girl popped out his cock and started sucking on it right there in front of me. Another girl joined her, and the girls on my side of the limo looked at me. Needless to say, we entered Denny's a little later than expected, and then they dropped me off back at my car at 6:00 a.m.

I then realized that this guy lived in a totally different world than most people. It was an amazing experience, and it also led me to gain the knowledge needed to write this book.

Dancers Are Dreamers

Most dancers are in la-la land when it comes to the reality of what they can really accomplish in life. They will tell you what they're going to do and all these grandiose plans they have. In all actuality, they are extremely lazy and want and have most things handed to them. Look at the way they earn a living. They talk to and grind on men who seek a fantasy world. Along with this, many of these girls are pathological liars. They have so much bullshit they feed guys, they don't really know who they are anymore. They put up walls as barriers. I noticed this mostly as I spent several nights with the same girls. I realized how much their stories changed every time they told them. If it is not the truth, you can't remember who you tell what.

It can be as simple as how much they made that night. They would tell me they were broke but then tell the stripper in the change room how they made two hundred dollars already. The sad part is that probably neither story was true. They probably had 150 bucks in their purse at the beginning of the night and now have 200 but don't remember what's what because they are high. The few exceptions to the rule are the businesswoman-type strippers. They are like an accountant or a Texas hold 'em player. They always know what they've made and where they rank among others. They have higher goals in general. Whether it is to buy a new car or a new purse, they go into every night with an expectation of what they want to make. Once they hit that number, they will probably slow down hustling.

As I mentioned in another section, if you go in later in the night, it gives you a better chance to get in cheap. After the strippers have made their money, they are looking for a good drink and some decent conversation.

Back to the dreamers. Just realize that you probably don't fit into their world long term, so don't go in with that expectation. You will see in the next section it's best to just have fun and don't expect much from most of these dancers, because most of them live in a world far from reality.

IV. Understanding You and the Top Mistakes You Won't Want to Make

Now that you understand the environment and the types of dancers and their mentality, let's look at you.

Smaller groups succeed better

Go to the strip club with no more than two to four guys. The reason smaller groups succeed better is that you aren't perceived as a bachelor party by the club. Dancers know that those guys are there to spend money on the groom and themselves, so it attracts a certain type of dancer. The businesswoman or the prostitute will jump all over these groups of men. When you see these guys come in, look at the girls going up to them. Make a mental note of those exotics, and stay away from them. I've had the best luck picking up dancers when I have gone in with only one other guy. You won't seem like this desperate lonely guy wanting to spend money on a girl if you have a wingman. Go in with a partner in crime and the mentality that you're there to have fun and are there truly to be entertained by the girls, instead of going in with the mindset of getting stuck in the money trap with these strippers, wondering how much you're going to get milked for at the end of the night.

They are there to try to bleed as much out of you as possible. They can only do this if you let them. Throw your expectations out the door. Expectations will only lead to disappointment in most cases. Most of the successes I had, really getting in deep at a club, came when I had one friend with me who really knew me well. This way, we could play off each other and joke around. All women like to laugh. Most of my friends were face men. I was always the hustler and entertainer. This combination works well, because my buddies would reel them in with their looks, and I'd go in stealth mode and lock them up. You don't want to go there with a guy who is too good-looking, because then the dancers could feel insecure and stay clear of him and you. There has to be a warm, inviting look to you both, perceived by the dancers. If you come across as judgmental or cocky, you will go home empty-handed. Trust me, I have been with all types of men in the strip club, working my magic, and if I can spot which guys are assholes, so can strippers, easily.

Dress for Success

From the perfect hat to trendy clothes to smelling of a nice cologne, you will want to put your best foot forward. The two main rules are: first, don't look dirty, and second, don't smell. That's true going into any bar and going up to all women. Some guys will overdo it with suits or cologne. I like to stay in the middle of the road. You want the dancers close to you and turned on by the way you smell. Do not drown them in it either. Buy a cologne that is trendy for the times. Don't wear Old Spice or Brut and expect the twenty-two-year-old not to think of their dad or even worse, their grandpa. You should purchase Polo or Timberlake's new one, something fresh and from the decade we live in.

Have you ever noticed baseball players all look good until they take their hats off? Wear a hat if you have a bad-shaped head or receding hairline. Personally, I'm balding with a decent-shaped head, but a hat takes five years and plenty of wrinkles off me. I'm just saying that if you dress a little younger and look a little more trendy, it will go a long way. It's the little things that help make you jump a point or two on the looks scale. If you're a four, you can jump to a six or seven easily with a certain look and smell. If you have bad breath, that can be a deal-breaker too. Coffee or cigars are a don't! Just chew gum and drink liquor, baby! Wearing black always helps slim the waistline. In the black lights, it will trim you up if you're a little chubby, but be careful of white lint or soap suds still embedded in the cotton. It will light up like a Christmas tree from those lights. You don't want to look fuzzy.

Dress clothes seem too businesslike, and therefore send the message: *I've got money to spend.* You don't want to be perceived that way. Plus, the groups I've seen who go in there after business meetings end up blowing a ton of money, and dancers are totally hounding those guys. Usually, their ego is in the way with their colleagues, and they end up spending way too much money. Why would you want to go in and blend in with that group anyway? That's why jeans or khakis or shorts are fine, but no ties and sport coats are necessary.

Eye Contact and Smiling Are Your Friend and Foe

We've all heard this before. In the stripper world, they will approach you even if you're not looking at them. Why give them an open invitation and make it even easier to show your interest in them by staring? If you make too much eye contact with them, they will be on you like stink on shit. Be careful here. You don't want to get sucked into this trap. If you don't have a problem saying no, then look all you want. If you do have trouble rejecting them, then you better choose wisely who you stare at.

One trick I use if I get caught staring at a girl I don't want to approach me is to say, "I thought you had blonde hair before," if it's dark and vice versa. This way, it gave you a reason to stare but a way out from having them come and sit down on you. I always tell them I like blondes or brunettes (the opposite of what they are) if I want them to leave.

I was called out one time on this, though. A dancer came up to me and asked me if I would like a dance. I said, "No, thanks, I prefer dances from black girls only." Holy shit! What are the odds that her roommate was black! She said, "Oh, you will love my roommate then." She went over and grabbed her roommate, and that exotic proceeded to sit on my lap. That cost me a drink and fifteen minutes of my time. It was fine, but I could clearly tell they were just in it for the money. Of course, rent was probably due, and her friend was making sure she would make enough money that night to cover it. I did have a great time being challenged by these dancers that night, though.

In most cases, when I think I have an answer for everything or a way out of a dance, something new pops up. Even worse is when a dumb dancer won't take the hint and leave, and you're stuck trying to figure out your exit strategy with her. You're probably thinking,

Why would you ever want a stripper to leave? We usually have to work so hard to get them to stay. Trust me, once you get comfortable with this new mindset in the strip club, you're going to realize we have the option of which strippers we want to engage with and get to know better outside the club. They will be at our mercy, not the other way around. After a while, you're going to agree with me that there are some girls who are so ridiculously dumb that you will avoid seeing them at all cost. There are plenty of guys I've met in my life who fall in this same category. Usually when I see this at the strip club, it's just that the girls are so drunk, they don't make any sense, so that's why I avoid them.

Getting Comfortable and Gaining Confidence When You Arrive

The most important thing here is to know and understand your surroundings. The first time I went to a gentlemen's club was awful. I sat along the back wall, and it was obvious that I looked and felt uncomfortable. It was clear that I knew how nothing worked in there. Dancers on their tip walk came up, and I was fumbling around in my pockets, searching for a dollar. I was fucking pitiful!

When you arrive, you must find your spot and get comfy. Order a drink. If you smoke, grab an ashtray and ask the bartender for a light. Ask her name with a smile and appear friendly. I'm not a smoker, but my friend was, and this worked to his advantage more often than not. He would have strippers stop by and ask him for a drag or a light because they smoked. I used to bring a pack and put it on the table, even though I didn't smoke, just to entice them. It definitely led to a few phone numbers for me the easy way. I think I still have that stale wrapper with a few left somewhere. Just kidding.

These days, every place is smoke-free, so the dancers go outside, and I don't use that angle anymore. What a great icebreaker, though, in a non-threatening way. Just ask them if they would like to grab a smoke outside with you, and you are off to the races. After they get to know you're a nice guy a bit, you will be banging them in no time. The last thing you want is for them to think you have the blacked-out-window kidnapper van outside.

When you have the environment down,

you will appear more confident, like you have done this before or you're a regular at other clubs. That reminds me: become a regular at a couple of clubs nearby. Most of these girls get mad or don't show up and jump from club to club. They might start out at a bikini club and move to a full-nude bar. They go in thinking they will make more money at a nude club, but in actuality, it depends on the girl. If the fees are higher and their cut is higher, they can make more, but it is all about the hustle. It's like sales. If you hustle, it doesn't matter where you are or what you are selling. If you're smooth, you're smooth.

Another point to make about having confidence while you're in the club is that you should only lie about yourself if you really feel comfortable doing it. Hey, look, we didn't place our right hand on the Bible and get sworn in when we paid our cover charge. Those girls' real names aren't Diamond and Porsche either! Strip clubs are about entertainment and escapism. Be who you want to be; just don't get caught in lies if you can't remember what you tell different dancers. They will forget by the next time you're in there, most likely, but still you gotta hang in there that night.

Be Ready for Her Signs

There is nothing worse than having a girl throw you signals and you're not ready or smart enough to figure it out. These girls do get rejected by broke guys regularly but not rejected when they are throwing themselves out there for free. So if you play the game right and they open the door to get to know you outside the club, jump all over it. The trap that you don't want to fall into—but you will find out soon enough—is that for every guy they are fucking, they have seven other guys who do shit for them.

If you're a computer guy or a car guy, don't—and I mean *don't*—offer shit for free. It works to get to know them better, but not if you want to fuck them. If, after a couple times you hang out with them and no play comes out of it, cut your losses and move on to the next girl at the club. She will probably tell the others what a nice guy you are and sell you to them at worst. If she does ask you why you don't hang out with her at all anymore or answer her calls, just explain that you're not looking for any more friends. Tell her you don't mind going slow and that you do respect yourself and her, but you need some kind of action, even if it's just kissing and touching.

Guys, let me tell you this: I've never met a stripper—or any woman, for that matter—who could hold off after you start making out with them. If they are enjoying it, they won't have the willpower to stop! You don't want to come across as desperate or pathetic. Remember to stay confident. Chances are, she will come back around after you move on politely. Once the competition starts with the other girls, she will be saying how you came over a month ago, and this and that, trying to seem cool, like you were interested and she denied you because of a boyfriend at the time or something. Like she was a good, trustworthy girl. Yeah, right. These girls can be so full of shit sometimes. It's ridiculous.

Jealousy Has No Place in a Strip Club

One thing I've learned is that jealousy won't work to your favor in here. Sometimes girls like to be chased or be shown that someone actually cares what they do, but in the club, they are there to make money. If we are there to get them for free, we have to allow them to wander to other guys and make their money from those other suckers. I actually tell them and help them spot suckers who are in there to blow money. The girls actually thank me and like to hang around me more for more insight if I help them spot the old guys who are not threats to them. The rookies and newer girls are the ones who need the most help anyway. Those are our main targets to begin with! The businesswomen already know who to target, and we stay clear of them in most cases.

Jealousy is very hard to hide after you have slept with a stripper, especially if a week later, she blows you off at the club. Just because you fucked doesn't give you possession rights. If you are that guy who can't suppress those negative feelings, go to a different club and stay clear of her and her club until you get over it. You will only hurt your reputation with other strippers if this girl dogs you out to her fellow strippers. You'll set yourself back six months in there if you go in and act jealous and bad-mouth her. No matter what, strippers are empathetic to other strippers before they will ever trust your word against hers, unless they don't like that girl already. My advice to you if this happens is always be nice and sound happy for her if she just used you, or go hang out at a different club if you hang your green-eyed monster on your sleeve.

Being Too Pushy Creeps Them Out

When have you ever seen a jerk make out with the girl? In high school, maybe this worked because reputations mattered then. Now that we are in the real world, jerks get thrown out! This just in: strip clubs are not the real world. But you know what I mean. I like the nice- but-confident-guy role. You have to come across like you have options in there at all times. The strippers do! You'd better be able to name-drop and know a few of the other dancers. You don't want to seem like a player, but you'd better have a confident approach to what you are looking for and what you want from them. You do this by talking, not grabbing or feeling your way into them. It can be a fine line between being aggressive and being a dick, but if you don't ask, you shall not receive either.

These girls are very used to being gawked at and complimented and grabbed. You definitely have to find a new, different approach to making a lasting impression.

I like to use laughter to make an impact. I'll make fun of myself or something in the club that doesn't make sense. I'll play off my buddies and talk about funny movies we want to see. What an easy tie-in to a non-threatening date. Tell a stripper a group of you are going to see the new Vince Vaughn movie or something and that you'd love to take her with and get to know her. She will not feel pressure at all. All you're trying to do is spend the most time with her without spending all of your money to do so.

This strategy has worked for me several times. I'll give you other angles in the Strategies section of this book. At the end of the day, you just want to come across as confident and sure of yourself without being too pushy or suggestive in what you would really like to do to them. Let's face it: every girl you've been extremely nice to in life, you've wanted to sleep with. It's just that some guys are less obvious at first about these actions. That's how you need to be with these girls!

Having the Patience of a Snail

This is very important in moving forward with these girls. Most of all, relationships stem from timing. These types of girls especially have no concept of time and usually have more drama than the average girl. It is very important for you to be very understanding and have minimal or very low goals and expectations with these women.

Generally speaking, dancers are unaccountable as hell. They are a different breed than the normal girl you would date. Lower the bar that you are used to, and you'll be less disappointed. It is directly related. The lower the class of girl, the lower the expectations you should have. Don't expect anything more or better than the quality of people you deal with. These girls are mostly from the bottom of the barrel. There are exceptions to every rule, and you might find the diamond in the rough, but get that silly thought out of your head.

I met a dancer a few years ago, and she gave me her number, and we talked and sent a few texts. This went on for weeks. I guess I had become so nonchalant with previous girls that I never asked her to do anything.

She sure as hell wasn't going to initiate a date. Then finally, her girlfriend at the club came up to me and asked if I had a girlfriend. I said no. She said, "Then why haven't you asked my friend out?" I thought about it for a second and said I wasn't sure if she could handle a guy like me yet and I was assessing her. She laughed and said, "Trust me, she can and wants to handle you."

It was a great answer to what I threw out there, but after I thought about it, I realized that I had become too patient with these girls and needed to get back to being more confident. That's the fine line we walk, because I almost lost my window of opportunity with her. Needless to say, we ended up going out and laughing about it in the end. Her friend joined us one night, since I made her laugh so much too. The one constant thing I did was I always continued to flirt, which caused her to always stay interested. So if that helps you any, feel free to try that.

You Can't Be Condescending

Look, these girls know what they do isn't brain surgery. They don't need you judging them or making remarks that make them feel even worse. I mentioned earlier that most stripper types don't tell family or close friends where they work. Their mom might know, for safety reasons, or think they are just a cocktail waitress at a strip club, but most of the time they don't go bragging about how they make their money. It's like being a drug dealer. They all get caught or busted out over time but want to hide it as long as possible.

I had one friend who always put down the girls when we'd be talking to them. He thought he was being funny by talking down to them. He joked about how they've once again made a bad decision, besides working at a strip club, by sitting down with us. It was truly funny, but it never once got us laid or the girls' phone numbers. The dancers weren't like, "Thanks for judging me and my decisions. Now let's go outside and I'll blow you." All it did was cause barriers and walls to go up that took forever to knock back down. I would go in a week or two later, and the girls would remember me and bust my buddy out. I was guilty by association. I learned two things from this: first to wait longer before going back in there and second to stop hanging out with that guy or any other wingmen who put down the girls.

V. Strategies and Approaches to Better Success

Interviewing the Dancer to Size Her Up

Right off the bat, when the stripper comes up to you and asks if you would like a dance, tell her they can sit down and talk to you first, and you'll consider a dance if the conversation goes well. Tell her you like to get to know a hot girl before you let her grind on you. She'll get a kick out of that at least and tell the other dancers if she doesn't sit down. This way you get to see if they are hustling or if they are there to have fun too. The girls who move on? You don't want to waste your time on them anyway. You will still have to weed out the exotics who do sit down, but at least now you get five or six minutes to interview them. Here's the deal: you have to get out of your head that you are there to see them. Reverse that shit. These girls are here to find out if you are the fucking man or not. You're the prize, not these dancers. I'm not trying to sound like a misogynist. I'm just saying you are both there for a reason. They fulfill your fantasy, and you fulfill your reality. I want you to mesh the two together and not just end up getting teased all night.

Let's face it: you are not the most upstanding, law-abiding citizen either, hanging out at a strip club. The funny thing is, when you bring your girl in there—who thinks all strippers are nasty and want to fuck you—you realize real fast it's a hell of a lot easier to pick up a girl at a normal club than to hit on a girl who knows how to reject a man by one look. Your girl and your conservative buddies will learn that the strip club is pretty much like a normal bar, just that the girls wear a lot less clothes and get paid to show you a preview of the goods. This is exactly how you need to view the strip club.

Most people think that the strip club is different than a normal bar. Look how very similar the two scenes are. Girls go there to dance, and guys go there to watch. Everyone drinks too much. Everybody wants to fuck. The biggest difference—and similarity—is that you only have twenty girls to hit on and a lot more guys you compete with. A normal bar has far more fatties and ugly girls, so the differences may seem big, but in all actuality, these two scenarios are more alike than different.

Setting Realistic Goals for the Opportunity that Presents Itself

You can't go into a club the first time and expect to bring the girl home. Unless you look like George Clooney or David Beckham, set realistic goals. The first time I go into a club, I try to make friends with one bartender. Buy her a shot or ask her favorite drink, and when she needs one throughout the night, tell her you'd like to buy it for her. She'll appreciate that and remember you. As long as you come across as the nice guy and not the creepy guy, she will stick up for you with the other dancers. If they ask, "Who is that guy hanging around?" she will be more likely to put in a good word and recommend you if you start off on her good side. Chances are, if it's a slow night, you'll talk to her more than a dancer. This is good news.

She will have the lowdown on everything in that club. Ask her which strippers give other girls better lap dances. You might be wondering, *why do I want to know the answer to that question?* The answer is if a stripper knows how to give really good lap dances to women, she probably likes women and could be a lesbian. See? Now you have eliminated strippers who will waste your time.

The bartender might tell you straight out who's lesbian, but this is a nice, subtle way for you to learn. Remember, I think a lot of guys go in trying to find the hottest dancer and try to get her number and usually get blown off, wasting a bunch of time. My approach of eliminating girl after girl narrows it down to maybe only having three to five potential targets. Now you can spend minimal time and money on the few girls you stand the best chance with. Make sense?

Use a combination of these techniques, assessing what type of stripper she is, and after networking to learn as much as you can about the girl, set a realistic goal with her.

This will let you really narrow your search down and have a plan.

The exception to the rule: Just like when a blind squirrel comes upon a nut every once in a while, sometimes you'll get lucky. The timing will be right with the girl, and she will just trust you automatically, or that particular stripper might be more adventurous. Absolutely go in for the same-night fuck if you can. These girls are so inconsistent and live such hectic lives, you may never see her in that club again. Take advantage of her weakness that night or the strong connection you might have made by closing the deal.

Buying Her a Drink

The dancers are taught to get you to buy them drinks. The dancers get a cut of what you buy for them. Usually they will get a ticket per drink, which at the end of the night they cash out for money. If the girl is under twenty-one, she won't order Coke or tell you. She'll just get a glass of water or Coke, and they'll charge you $7.50 for it. Its total bullshit and a complete rip-off. The smart girls will hang out and talk and ask for a drink, even if you turn down a dance, because they can easily pay tip out during the week from drink tickets alone. The strategy here is to go to the club later in the night, like at eleven or midnight, after they have made enough to cover tip out. You increase your chances of scoring if they're not worried about covering that.

I use buying the girls a drink as a strategy a lot if they are over twenty-one, because it is a great, cheap way to spend two to three times the amount of time with them versus a general lap dance. You just have to be careful you're not buying water or orange juice. The easy way to recognize this if is if the girls constantly leave half their drinks behind. Granted, they didn't pay for it to begin with, but who leaves a perfectly good Jack and Coke behind?

Asking for a Meeting Outside the Club

Dinner, lunch, breakfast—it's what I've used and what works best. Here is the mistake I see time and time again from my buddies. They go in and meet the new girl and buy her a drink. They let the girls talk, and they do everything right but close the deal! They ask if they can get the girl's number and take her out to dinner or a movie, some traditional type of date. Ugh, this kills me. These strippers are far from regular. They use their bodies to tease and manipulate you, all to get your hard-earned money! Then most of the dancers brag to their colleagues or friends how they took you for five hundred bucks.

The strategy that works best is to let them suggest what they would like to do. Most girls are shy and want the guy to decide, which is fine, but make it interactive. What I like to do is ask if they would like breakfast after a shift that night or possibly later on that week, because they might need to get home to a babysitter that night. When you get off work, do you go straight to bed? I didn't think so. See, these girls don't go straight to bed after their shift just because it's late. They eat and probably shower and watch TV to unwind before bedtime at 6:00 a.m. That's why breakfast at Denny's or wherever is cheap and public (which equals safe in their world) and is your best place to get to know them.

Have them bring another dancer if possible. They might do that regularly anyway, and if it was a slow night, they might appreciate you buying breakfast. But look at the return on investment! Thirty bucks for breakfast with one or two dancers, for a ninety-minute meal! Wow! You can't buy one lap dance for three minutes for that price. Even if they have a boyfriend, kind of (and all dancers "kind of have" a lot of things), it's just the guy they're fucking that month! The girl who has a serious boyfriend won't agree to join you for breakfast, most likely.

Let's get back to the mistake my friends make. If you ask them to lunch, they usually sleep past noon, and dinnertime is bad, because before their 8:00 or 10:00 shift, they won't want to get bloated or chubby before wearing a thong all night. There is a window of opportunity around 3:00 p.m. that will work, but you probably have a job too, so that kills that. On their days off, they probably won't spend time with you just yet—until they like being around you! Remember, you have knowledge and wisdom over them, not just money. They only see the money at first. But my approach to breakfast at first is just a smooth, proven, easy way to get to know them fast and cheap. Even if you're not attracted to them that much, it will be a great way to make friends with the strippers at the club, and they can sell you to future prospects.

Gathering Information from Other Dancers on Dancers You're Interested In

You will have better success rates this way and know which exotics to avoid. I just mentioned in the last section that these girls are your moles. Even if they just tell you stories about other dancers, you constantly have to be making mental notes on each girl. I know that remembering their stage names and real names can be like a pharmacist remembering generic drugs versus branded drugs, but at least you need to be making notes on the bad prospects to avoid. The same few girls' names will be popping up from the other girls on how they cut in on their regular or hustled in the bachelor party that just walked in. Those are exactly the girls you need to avoid. *Hustler stripper* seems redundant, but there are a few in every club. Most of the dancers are just lazy, lazy, lazy! That's what you want. I mean, look at how these girls make a so-called living. They earn money for barely grinding on you. Most dancers are minimalists. They will do just enough to survive. There is the occasional hustler who is the businesswoman and has a house or nice things to keep up. Generally those girls find the rich guy to support that lifestyle eventually, though. I know at least one dancer per club I've been into who supports herself. Let me be clear—who *actually* supports herself. Many will tell you this but they're full of shit!

Regularity—Going to the Same Club Over and Over Again

In earlier sections, I mentioned building a network and learning as much as possible about the dancers. The key thing to remember here is that many dancers change clubs regularly, so you don't have to. Lots of these girls travel from an hour away, so they are not recognized in their hometown. This is good because then they won't hear about *your* local reputation either. There might be a few girls there who have been there a long time (two-plus years is a long time in their world), but don't worry about them. Overall, after a few months of working there, girls are going to come and go, so you don't have to.

I noticed this the first time after I didn't go to a club by my house for six months. I was in a relationship and didn't go in for a while, and then when I eventually went in, everything had changed. The manager changed, and the bartenders were new. Half the dancers didn't look familiar. The beautiful thing was that the doorman was the same guy, and the hen was the same. They both remembered me, and I remembered their favorite drink. By the end of that one night, I had the scoop on who was new, what happened to the old manager, which girls were hustlers, and most importantly, who my next targets were! I have been to more than twenty different strip clubs. Only half of these I've been to more than once. I'd said only about five or six of them I've spent the time needed to build a network. Three of these have been the main ones I've done damage in. It's like the 80-20 rule: 80 percent of the girls come from 20 percent of the clubs. Just like in sales. I guess the key thing is that from the multiple types of clubs I've been to, the smaller-name, rural-area clubs have worked the best for me. The quality of girl is one to two points lower overall on a scale of ten, but who are we kidding? We aren't Brad Pitt either, or we wouldn't need this book to help us!

Networking in the Club

Bartenders, wait staff, even bouncers are your friends. You need to build up credibility with them. The easiest way to build your credibility in the club is to network. These strippers are skeptical about every guy who comes in there. If you can drop a few names of staff that you hung out with, or that you know a bouncer pretty well, this will go a long way. Even if you saw them at a softball game or you are friends with the bartender. You will build street credibility. You will achieve a safety association with these people, which is what the stripper is looking for. All women want to feel safe with the guy they are with. So if you have signs of desperation or being too eager, that will just creep them out and shy them away. Coming on too strong or pushy is probably the biggest mistake most men make. Safety holds true with all women in all environments.

Every book I've read and every girl I've talked to says safety is the number-one feeling they need to have, to go out on a date with you. So you cannot look, feel, smell you-name-it and appear unsafe if you want to get to the next level. If you do appear unsafe for any reason, you are done! You will have no chance with any girl, including exotics. Avoid topics on the news of girls being abducted or negative issues at all; you don't want these girls associating you with anything negative or creepy. Talk about vacation spots or fancy meals or shopping—romantic and safe topics only.

Strippers Outside the Club

Let me explain that I always thought that girls acted the same outside the club as they do inside the club. These girls are entertainers, and most of the time turn it on and turn it off. At least the businesswomen do. They really try to keep things totally separate and are more willing to blow you off at the mall or at Target than actually acknowledge you. Don't take it personally if they do avoid you. A better approach to use is the next time you're at the club, when you see them again, say you saw them out in public. Mention that you noticed them but didn't want to catch them off guard outside the club. They will appreciate your sensitivity to this matter of privacy, and in return you will earn big-time street credibility with them in trusting you.

If they say "next time say hi" and that they don't care, then you are good to go. At that moment, it might be a good time to invite them to meet you at the mall sometime. Tell them you need help picking out a shirt for a wedding and would like their opinion. They will love the subtle, smooth way you asserted yourself. Please understand that outside the club, they don't dress like that. Most guys think that they dress slutty and half-naked outside the club. It is also assumed that they wear thong swimsuits all the time to the beach. That is generally not true. Some of the girls who are starving for attention will wear riskier clothes, but generally they get so much attention at the strip club, they don't want attention drawn to them at Wal-Mart.

Hit the Strip Club at the End of the Night

Go in the last hour the club is open. First of all, you won't be there long enough to spend too much money. Secondly, some of the dancers will have made their money for the night and want to relax a little. You have to spot the ones who have done this. The ones who haven't covered tip out yet are looking for the drunk sucker who's been drinking all night and now will open his wallet to them. Make sure you're not that sucker. It's pretty easy to ask them if they've had a good night. They will tell you. If they have had a good night, offer them a drink to relax and have a good conversation. It'll cost you a lot less, and trust me, they are tired of guys yelling and grabbing at them all night and will enjoy a real person interested in getting to know them. Little do they know you're trying to get more than just a lap dance out of them.

Watch Out for the End of the Month

Car payments and rent are due. They might be hustling to get that knocked out and paid for. Don't fall into that trap. It goes along with going to the strip club at the end of the night. After they made their money on other victims, you swoop in to get them when they are not stressed about covering their nut they've got to pay. It reminds me of speeding in your car at the end of the month. Some cops have a quota to hit and use radar more at the end of the month. Strippers do the same. They hustle more to pay rent or car payments the last few days of the month. The weekend girls do the same, on the whole. That's why weeknights work best to pick up girls. It's slower in the club, so more time for you to build the friendship. However, you could get targeted more too, so if you have trouble saying no to girls, watch out for this trap. I'll give you some strategies and replies to use to get out of dances in the next section.

The Mature Man Has a Better Approach than the Twenty-One-Year-Old

This alludes to the concept that you have had more practice at getting rejected or accepted by women. The key here is that what works with one woman might not with another. Also, just because you're forty years old versus twenty doesn't mean you have learned anything from your previous advances with women. Confidence doesn't always come with age or beauty. Actually, the most really good-looking men and women tend to be the most insecure. This is because we are always trying to achieve their personal best. I always try to reach my ideal body weight and fat percentage like when I was twenty-eight. That's not going to happen anymore.

What I learned to do and what has worked the best in certain situations, I've repeated time and time again. If the wheel isn't broken, don't try to fix it. Twenty years of failed experiences don't make you any better than the young guy with one year of failed experiences. If you adapt those twenty years of experiences and approaches to your style and recognize the different types of women and cater to those, you will have created the formula for victory. Whether you are young or old, guys who have created a formula for success will never sleep alone. That's why it is so important to set goals and find small victories each night.

Rejection is tough enough to swallow. No matter how many times I've gotten shot down or laughed at, I've just learned to not take it personally. It could be for a number of reasons. They could be lesbian or married or banging the owner. It barely has anything to do with you—unless you remind them of their dad. If anything, pretty girls don't get hit on as much as you think. Most good guys are intimidated. The jerks will try, and the strippers get frustrated with those losers as much as we do seeing them try. That's out in public mostly. At the strip club, every guy with a hard-on flirts with them. Dancers are mostly immune to guys at the club hitting on them. That's why your advances have to be smoother and more thought out. And above all, timing is everything!

Ways Out of Getting Roped into Dances

One thing I like to do when a girl comes up to me and asks for a dance is simply say, "No thanks, I'm just drinking tonight." If the girl seems a little persistent, just say you prefer dances from someone of the opposite hair color or name a girl you're waiting for from earlier in the night. All are sure signs and easy ways out of getting suckered in. The big key here is not to make the initial long eye contact to begin with that initiates her advances. That is your way of inviting them over to begin with. It is tough because you want to check them out but not look obvious enough to want them to come over. Usually I'll just grab my phone and pretend to text or Facebook or something, to seem uninterested in lap dances altogether.

If I am interested in a girl but don't want to spend money on a lap dance from her, I'll just say, "I'm not interested in a dance, but if you come by after you give other dances, I'll buy you a drink, and I would like to get to know you better." This way you're throwing it out there that you're interested and leaving the door open for her to come back and hang out if she's interested in you. Hey, as well as I can handle rejection, it's still nice not to have it thrown directly in my face. This way, if they do come back, you know you're initially in the door. If they don't come back, then you know they were just interested in making money that night or got sidetracked. Don't take it personally.

Strippers Want What Other Strippers Have

If you're wanted by one stripper, it will lead to others wanting you. I first realized this when I showed interest in a primo dancer and she wouldn't give me the time of day. She was all about the money, and I wasn't shelling it out. I spent time networking in the club, and my reputation grew as a normal, cool, regular guy. Believe it or not, there are a ton of weird whack jobs who go in there. Other girls started asking about me. They wanted to know what I liked about a certain girl. I started to see that if I showed interest in one stripper, the other dancers' curiosity would grow. I figured out that even if I wasn't very interested in a less-attractive stripper, it would springboard me to get the dancers I wanted.

I used one stripper who was a complete mess to eventually get the girl I wanted. She was very hot but just all over the place mentally. After I took that girl out and didn't sleep with her, my street credibility grew. She was selling me to all the other girls. She told them I had a good job and a nice car. I just played off that. I traveled a lot and eventually would take her out again. The strategy I used here worked because when I went back in on a night that the train wreck wasn't working, I said hi to some of the girls who were her friends. I mentioned I took that other girl out. It spread like wildfire in the club.

Later on, the girl I initially showed interest in who blew me off came up and asked for a tip. I said, "Here's your tip," and proceeded to mention that I should have taken *her* out instead of that train wreck. She laughed hard at what I said and sat down to talk. I explained to her that the girl was nice but just not my type; I gave her a few reasons why, but nothing too negative. Then I said with confidence, "When we eventually go out, I hope you're taking notes now so our date goes better." She didn't give me her number just yet, but I got her laughing and considering me. Then I basically told her to go make money on other guys, and if she wanted to continue our conversation later, she could stop back by or give me her number outside the club. Sure enough, she came back by with her number, and she was all smiles.

The key here was that I left her wanting more. It was something most guys had never done or tried before. It was original. Most of these exotics run from the guys in the club after they get their lap dance money out of them. Sometimes they run off to find other men to make more money on, or possibly because that guy creeped them out. In this case, she knew I could be trusted because I took the other dancer out before, and things went fine.

These girls are very competitive; she didn't care if I slept with that other girl or not. Normal girls always rule you out if you slept with someone they know. Those rules don't apply to strippers. When I ended our conversation and told her to go make money, it did two things. It let her know she wasn't going to make money on me, but it also showed that I was interested in her as more than a friend by asking her to consider going out with me. It's always a gamble, but isn't that what we're doing here? Trying to weed out the ones who just want to use us for money.

VI. Personal Tales from the Clubs

My First Real Experience at the Club

How I built up my confidence in a strip club from having comfort. Let me start off by saying that other than being more scared of being arrested at a strip club with my fake ID at the age of nineteen, I had never had any comfort level in a strip club before this experience. Then one Saturday night, the boys and I, about seven of us, went to the dog track. We were drinking and winning. It was a great time, and I was barely twenty-two years old. Most of the guys were in their late twenties and had more experience at the bars and strip clubs in general. We decided to hit the local strip club on the way home from the dog races.

We walked in, and this was my first time to this club. It was my first experience in a topless girl bar. I had been to a few bikini strip clubs before, but that was it. Naturally, I was excited just to see boobs for free! Our group grabbed a table and sat down and admired the surrounding twenty half-naked girls. A couple of the dancers saw our group and headed over to hustle us. I remember one girl in particular who had the perfect set of natural tits and a small ass, my personal favorite combination and weakness, mind you. She introduced herself as Dillon and pulled up a chair to sit down and talk with us. She probably figured that eventually someone in our group would want a dance and that the numbers were in her favor.

We ordered a round of drinks, and she ordered herself a drink on her own tab, which I appreciated, because she seemed to not be in any rush to just hustle us for money. Our group was busting each other's balls about life, and she was laughing and listening to our childhood stories and carrying on. She fit in like she was just one of the guys. Our antics couldn't offend her, which was nice, and we joked around about anal sex with women. Truly, it was an all-around learning experience for me. She got up from the table to do a few featured dances on stage when it was her rotation. Also, she would give a lap dance now and then to other regulars that she ran into, but mostly she kept coming back to our table to talk and hang out.

Finally, my married friends were like, "Get her number. She's hot, and she likes you." At that moment, I decided to make my move. When she came back, instead of her sitting in the chair, I grabbed her waist and made her sit on my lap. She smiled and said, "You at least better rub my back if I'm going to sit here for free!" We all laughed, and I agreed. For the next thirty minutes, I continued to rub her back, and the guys were talking to her. I felt like a baller, just relaxing with this hot stripper on my lap enjoying herself. It was as fun as you can imagine, and nothing was paid for, and nothing dirty was going on.

At that moment, a few of the other strippers noticed Dillon and came over to our group, to see what was going on. She basically told them we were cool guys and to sit down and hang out and that they would have fun too. Two dancers sat down and began to joke with us. Now that the boys were loose and drunk and really having a good time, we all could take it up a notch. A couple of the boys went in the back and got lap dances and had a blast. The whole time, I just chilled and orchestrated the whole thing like a king with my queen sitting on my lap!

At the end of the night, I asked Dillon if I could call her and get to know her outside of the club. She told me she was seeing a guy but I could still have her number and to let her know when we were coming in again. At that point, she had worked there for two years, and she knew the deal about many of the dancers. Dillon was willing to endorse or warn me about them. In retrospect, I guess that moment was when I realized there is a whole other world out there in the strip club and that these girls can be fairly normal too.

She had a roommate she wanted to introduce me to, who ended up being the bartender who was off that night. In the next section, you will learn that that's who taught me how to build my network in the strip club, which led to this book. Dillon had that boyfriend for at least two years after that night, but as we all hung out in groups, she still is one of my most favorite dancers. The best part of that night with her on my lap is that she was wearing cocoa butter lotion. I awoke the next morning with my hands smelling of that lotion, and to this day, if I smell that scent, it brings me back to that night as if I was in a time machine.

The Bartender Who Launched Me to the Next Level in the Club

I was introduced to the bartender by Dillon, the dancer with the cocoa butter lotion who broke me in. I instantly hit it off with her, and we quickly became good friends. She had seen us in there before and heard us joking around and having a good time. One dancer was sitting at the bar with my buddy, and I and I asked the stripper if she liked anal sex. The bartender overheard us and chimed in, "I don't just like anal sex, I prefer it!" My mouth dropped. I knew right then and there this girl and I were going to become great friends. She was just like one of the guys and had heard and seen it all.

The bartender and I began to build our friendship. While the dancer was in between stage performances, I picked the bartender's brain and soon realized how much she knew about the infrastructure of the gentlemen's club. Also, she started telling me about the other girls and who was cool and who to stay away from. I hit the jackpot. Remember, I didn't have this knowledge of any kind of strip club previously. I was only around this scene for one month at this time. I absorbed her information like a sponge, listening to everything she said. Basically she taught me 50 percent of what I know about this lifestyle, everything from how the club makes money to how the girls spot suckers. She knew it all.

After a while, she told me how years ago she used to dance and travel around the country and that she did all of this by the ripe old age of twenty-two. I met her the following year. That first night we met, we exchanged numbers, and I told her I would call her to find out her work schedule so I could go in and see her again. She was nice to everybody at the club, and her personality was awesome. I didn't go into that friendship with her thinking or knowing that she eventually would teach me the ways of the samurai!

A few months later, she had a birthday party in Chicago. She invited my friends and me to join her and her girlfriends. Naturally, this meant several dancers, all outside the club, hanging out with us all at one time. You can imagine what that eventually led to. Now looking back, my friend and I rank it as one of the top five nights of my single life, hanging out with friends and partying in Chicago. Not only did we have a great dinner and dancing that night, we crashed at their condo and just lived the lifestyle you can only dream of.

After that night, other dancers invited us to their parties and to the summer festival in Milwaukee. We had a nice little rotation of stripper events that summer. As more girls would start dancing in the club and joining the group, we would be invited to more and more events. We kept that going for six months. It was awesome! Eventually the bouncers started inviting us to their parties. It was like the dancers would ask the bouncers if DP and company were going to be there. The bouncers would come over and basically beg me to show up. Of course I did, and I'd bring my boys along for the ride too.

One night that stands out the most is when this bouncer had a party at his farmhouse out in Bumfuck Egypt. Two friends and I followed them out there at 3:00 a.m. when the club closed. There must have been fifteen dancers and ten regulars from the club and a few others I didn't recognize. Things ended up a little crazy that night, so I'll jump forward to the good parts. My one friend ended up pressed against the back shed, making out with a stripper, with his pants down around his ankles. This farm dog was sniffing his ass while he was all over this girl. He was so drunk, he barely knew what was going on.

My other buddy and I were laughing our asses off watching him, while in the background this huge loud tractor drove by. I guess the farmer was doing something to move his massive stock of cows from one side of the farm to the other. It was close to 5:00 a.m. at this point. When we went back to the front of the house, we saw all these guys standing around a tall maple tree. They were all looking up in bewilderment. I looked at my buddy, S, and asked, "What's going on up there?"

Then we saw two naked strippers hanging in the branches, laughing, all drunk and acting crazy. Then the two bouncers who were hosting the party shook the tree, and all these bats came flying out everywhere; the two strippers were yelling and screaming.

They worked their way down the branches and eventually fell out of the tree. It was hilarious. I guess the bouncer dared them to climb up there naked, and the girls just thought it would be fun. The guys knew that the bats were up there, so when they shook the tree to scare the fuck out of them, it would surprise them. It worked, but it scared the shit out of all of us too! We ran to the back shed and grabbed my buddy, and we were like, "Let's get the fuck out of here."

Obviously, at the club the following week, we had a great story to tell. It was the talk of the club, and the story continued to help build our credibility with the other strippers moving forward. The point here is to keep an open mind and network, and you'll be happy you did. It will pay off in the long run.

Getting in with One Stripper Equals Getting You in with Many

This mostly happens when you find the right girl who is well-liked in the club. I've seen this work to your advantage and also possibly backfire on you. It could work either way. One club I spent many nights in had a few dancers who had their own clique. It was obvious the other girls were jealous and stayed clear of them. If the clique is a group of prostitutes and they feel you could steal business from them, those bitches will come after you in the bathroom and threaten you.

For the most part, exotics stick to themselves. They might have one or two dancers they carpool with, or they could be roommates with another girl. Their lives are so jacked up, they seem to try anything to survive, which is why they are there dancing in the first place. Definitely some strippers truly enjoy it and have fun with it. Most of them didn't start off that way. Your job is to spot the rookies and the uncomfortable girls who haven't seen it all yet. The dancers or staff who will get you the credibility you seek are the lifers or the bartenders who aren't really competing with those new fly-by girls you're after. I call them that because usually they don't dance long. It's a hard life. It's really easy money but not for everyone. Could you imagine having to hustle guys night after night by making small, meaningless talk for a few dollars?

When you do spend a few nights in the same club, these dancers will get easier and easier to spot just by where the bouncers hang out and the girls they talk to. You will be able to tell quickly who's who in the club. This is why networking under the radar is the key. You do not want to advertise that you are looking for cheap entertainment. Also, be careful not to advertise that, because guys like you are the owner's worst nightmare, the cheapskate who takes up table space and doesn't blow hundreds. The key is to still drink and talk. You paid your cover and have a right to hang out. You just want to appear like you're picky, not cheap. Especially if you are a mature man. None of the girls expect Johnny twenty-one-year-old to be blowing big bucks, but if you look established, it's assumed that that's why you're in there. The exotics assume you're there to see young, hot chicks and to buy dances, because clearly your old, fat, non-sexy wife isn't turning you on anymore. That's where these girls are wrong. Men are always horny, and it's like money—you never have enough to satisfy you!

We are there for the entertainment too. At least I am. My goals are just different now. It's like when I was younger; I tried to go to the bar and meet girls to get laid. As you get older, you realize that's not as hard as it used to be if you've learned anything throughout the years. Now when I go to the bar, my objective has changed. I like to find girls who will do threesomes or more wild and kinky stuff. For example, I hunt for girls who will have sex outdoors or possibly in public bathroom stalls. That's what drives me now. I've just raised my personal bar and expectations. It's like in golf. After you've played a few years you expect pars or birdies on par fives. Knocking in putts for bogeys doesn't make you happy like when you first started playing. Now back to the strategy.

Finding that right girl might be tougher because other men are vying for her time too. Other guys might be sitting at the bar, not knowing how valuable that bartender or dancer is, but they have a history with them. You may need to talk with that guy if he's approachable. He could be a nice guy, and if he is sitting alone, he might enjoy your company. Why not? Who says you can't be friendly with another customer? Most of those guys or girls are there because they are lonely and want a drink where it's acceptable to go alone. At the local bar down the street, it might be weird to be hanging by yourself at the bar. The main difference is these guys enjoy the scenery. If they were just drunks, they would not pay eight bucks a drink to get drunk. Instead they would just go to the local pub and drink for half the cost. Just remember, they aren't going to know what your goal is unless you tell them.

Bottom line: you're not doing anything wrong either. You are just trying to find value in the strip club and maximize your entertainment in the club that night. I just want guys to realize that maybe the expectation to have a good time in a strip club usually costs several hundred dollars, but that doesn't have to be the case at all. If you spot the right girl and approach her the right way, you will have a better, less expensive time and increase your chances of getting laid if you start to integrate these tactics into your game.

Strippers Are Competitive!

Okay, finally. I mentioned earlier how strippers want what other strippers have. I told you the story of how it worked to my advantage with the one stripper who turned me down at first, and then a month later she came back around, showing an interest in me after her colleague showed interest. Well, here's the continuation on that topic that digs deeper on how to play this to your advantage. At first, you might think this story belongs in the Strategies section, but after you read it, you will realize I was just along for the ride. The strippers made their mind up, and my friend and I benefited from it.

One night, I was hustling a dancer named Star and asked her to hang out with me on her night off. She was reserved at first and then kind of showed interest in hanging out with my buddy, S, who she'd met before. I never take things personally, so I mentioned I could hook her up with him, only if she would invite a friend who might like me. I also mentioned that throughout the night, she might reconsider her choice and that I could possibly grow on her. I just wanted her to keep an open mind and stay flexible. I like planting the seed. She agreed and said her roommate Alexis (who danced also) had Tuesday night off.

I called my buddy, S, and said I got two strippers lined up for Tuesday night so he should free up his schedule and that he would be thanking me on Wednesday for sure! Star and I exchanged numbers and decided to meet at the club for nickel draft beer night.

We could start off shooting pool, and then after we had had some cheap drinks in us, we could go bar-hopping and take things from there. Plus, I figured if they didn't show up, we could just work the Tuesday night B-team that generally works, since I had never been there on a Tuesday before. Sure enough, Star and Alexis showed up, and they looked hot. I had never seen Star in ripped jeans and a tank top with her hair down before. Alexis was sexy as hell too. A little bigger-busted than I like, but nonetheless, it was a great opportunity to build our street cred and create that competitive edge I talked about earlier. We ended up drinking and laughing and having a good time at the first place. Throughout the night, I asked Star if her friend was digging me and if she was having a good time. Star had mentioned that things were going well with her and Alexis and that she personally was physically more attracted to my buddy, S, but she had a great time laughing with me too.

I said, "No worries. My friend and I are having a great time and are attracted to both of you very much in all ways." This way you keep all the doors open. Don't shoot yourself in the foot by leaving options out. Star ate that shit up and told her roommate later on that they should invite us back to their apartment for drinks and fun. This is when the night turned, and these girls had made up their mind on having their way with us.

We left the last bar and followed them back to their apartment. They offered us some more drinks and were sitting around their coffee table when Alexis mentioned playing truth or dare. Obviously, this game was invented for everyone to end up naked and fool around, and that's exactly what happened. We went upstairs to Star's room and had a blast. I will leave the details up to your imagination. My friends know this is very hard for me to do. In person, I'm very graphic and detailed with my stories, but my mom will read this, so out of respect for her, I can't be a total pig!

The point I want to make about strippers wanting other strippers' lifestyles and being very competitive in all ways holds true. The dancer's roommate wanted her lifestyle and went along for the ride. She was fairly shy, so when the situation presented itself, she did like me. We kept an open mind and had fun with it. No jealousy, no inhibitions. I'm sure the gallon of booze we drank didn't hurt our chances either. We got a lot of mileage out of that story with our buddies and with other dancers. The girls who were not shocked by that story we knew we had a chance with. It led to more double dates down the road.

That reminds me of guys you meet who have lots of casual sex; that's what you wish you could be like, and you look up to them. You wonder how they do it and if you can learn to be like them. We become competitive with them or act just like them to see if we can pull that lifestyle too. That's exactly what happens here with these strippers. Don't let them fool you. Most of them are completely obsessed with their bodies and their looks. The new exotics try to keep up with the veteran dancers who make the most money and have the most guys chasing them. They want to be like them. If you are friends with her or have dated her, that gives you an edge with these rookies new to the club. As long as you didn't burn any bridges with that girl, you're golden. It's like in sales. I was always wondering how the top reps did it. I wanted to ride along with them and see if I could learn what they do well. If I copied them, then possibly I could sell as much as they did. That's what creates that competitive drive.

That's also why you will hear strippers talk about what other girls made in one night. Obviously they are doing this job for the money or to feed an addiction. Whether it's drugs or shopping, they're hustling guys for a reason. It's your job to figure out what angle you're going to use to get you in.

VIP status

When you first read this, you'll think it means the roped-off areas for special treatment, where people who spend a lot of money hang out. In some clubs, this is true. I'm going to describe a couple of different scenarios that I've been involved in that were referred to as VIP status. The first is when I was friends with the bartender at the main club where I hung out. I referenced her earlier. She told me about the club's VIP card. She obviously knew and saw that we were coming in regularly and told us how we could save money. At this particular club they had a couple of different levels, the silver VIP card and the gold VIP card. I believe they had platinum or diamond too. I never reached that status.

What was nice about buying that silver

VIP card, in addition to saving the entrance fee, is that it meant we were regulars. When new strippers (who were targets, remember) starting working at the club and I would show them the VIP card, along with knowing a bunch of other strippers, it gave me instant credibility. All of a sudden, it was like I worked there to them. I even started telling them which girls to stay away from. You see, I was able to flip their mentality. Usually, we are the ones getting roped into shit and taken for our money in those places. Now I had the power by telling the rookie good information in a non-threatening way. Those rookie girls were nervous too. This way, it was like I was a friend right off the bat, which went far in the end.

In the structure of a strip club section, when I calculated the savings of money from cover charges, it was nice, but this new value I received from the card of instant credibility with rookies is immeasurable. Basically, their perception is that I was the one who had the rundown on the club. Just like in the beginning, I was the rookie searching for the club's information, now I flipped that. I even helped the dancers know which guys would blow money on them and which jerks to stay away from. Even though these girls didn't give me dances that night or on future nights, when I made my move to ask them to dinner or a night out on the town, I had a very high success rate because of this tactic. I would find out their boyfriend status, kid status, which nights they were free, and what they liked to do, all before going in for the kill. It's like a good sales rep. Find the need first and then offer the solution. If you do your homework right, you can't lose. Closing becomes the easy part if you set yourself up for success.

Getting Invited to the After Parties as a Guy!

Once you've established you are a cool guy and a regular at the club, being invited to parties is much easier. Generally speaking, the bouncers will have an after-hours party with some of the dancers from the club. If you can get invited to this, you're golden. It's takes awhile to get to this status because those bouncers are trying to accomplish the same thing you are: getting laid for free. However, they might feel pretty confident you are not a threat and just a fun, friendly guy the girls feel safe around. I mentioned that bats-in-the-tree story from earlier. That was a bouncers' party, remember. That's the reputation you want to have. Occasionally the dancers will have people over after their shift, but not generally. Usually that situation will be small groups, not parties. Hot-tub parties are the best. I've never met dancers who had a nice place with a hot tub, but if you do, it's pretty much expected that you will end up naked and fool around. If you have a hot tub, it's better if you don't mention it until they get to your place. When they see it and get all excited, you'll know what their expectations are. If they don't want to get in, then it's more of a friendly visit at first. If the girls have suits in the car, then you know it's on!

Most strippers have a few outfits in their car because they're always coming and going from somewhere. It's like the girl who has condoms in her purse. Thank God she is safe, but you know she is having lots of casual sex if she comes prepared. Don't be surprised if you ask a girl back to your place and she brings a dancer and a bouncer too. It's just a way to make sure they are safe. This can actually work to your favor at the time you invite them over. Invite them to bring a dancer or friend with their boyfriend (who was probably in the strip club earlier) to your place. Tell that stripper she can invite a bouncer over that she might be interested in if it gets your prospect to agree to come over. Remember, these bouncers want to get in with strippers too and date or fuck them.

Your goal is to become allies with the bouncer, not compete with him. Some dancers, if they are attracted to the bouncer, will want to blow him instead of paying him tip out if they had a slow night. You better believe anything you can imagine will happen in this low-moral environment. I'll save some of this inside knowledge for the next book. I have too many stories to fit all in this book.

Having Better Luck in Small-Town Clubs and with Small-Town Girls

I've noticed that the small-town clubs and the clubs that are out in the cornfields off of truck routes seem to be the best clubs to pick up dancers. They are harder to get to and have less turnover, but nonetheless, the girls are fairly decent and easy to work. I like the clubs that are within forty-five minutes or so from where I live. I prefer fairly good-sized strip clubs that are located out in the boonies. This way you don't stand out to the girls, and you won't be easily remembered.

The strip clubs that have a main stage and two to three other side stages are perfect. Usually they will have a roped-off back area or VIP area and possibly a more secluded champagne room. There are usually about twenty to thirty girls working on a weekend night. That seems to be the average. Fifteen to twenty girls may be scheduled on a weekday night shift, but many seem to call off, since these are the slower nights. These are my favorite clubs to target because you have plenty of strippers to choose from, but since they don't get busted by cops as often, the exotics and bouncers seem to be more lenient. In the big cities, it's more of a hustle because more girls are working per shift. Sixty to seventy dancers will work a shift at VIP's in Chicago on any given night. The exotic dancers who work here will look like Playboy bunnies, but you have a lot of men competing and throwing big bucks at them for their time.

Another reason I like these smaller clubs with these types of girls that drive to be there is that if they finished school in their graduating class of forty, they generally won't be as picky with their choices in men. Think about it: any girl who only had twenty guys to choose from over four years of high school can't be that picky. Even if they dated older or younger guys, they still have limited options and probably liked or dated half the boys in the school. This is a good mentality for you. Less picky equals more willing to give you the time of day. Sounds like a win-win for you. The really small clubs, those I call hole-in-the-walls, I don't prefer. These are usually right by hotel chains or in downtown areas. These girls tend to be from out of town, but they are used to the businessmen traveling through who are willing to drop big money for dances or hand jobs and then go home to their wives. Many dancers in the 'prostitutes' category tend to work at these clubs by hotels. This way, if they like a guy, it's convenient for them after their shift to make some real money back at his hotel room. The stripper mentality kicks in here for the girls who have worked in a small club awhile. They develop a type of customer they expect walking in the door.

Again, that's why it's so important for you to find and approach the new girls who are nervous, remember. They don't have an expectation of the type of customer who comes in. This way, you can surprise them. That's why it is always important for you to frequent a club so you can spot the new talent. In my case, I knew the bartenders and bouncers well enough to ask them who the new strippers were and what the lowdown was on each one of them. I cast a very large net in my area because I had more friends who wanted me to take them out and teach them my successful strategies. I couldn't just go to the same three clubs. I had to use ten to fifteen clubs in my rotation. Hence, I'm writing this book for you to gain some of my insight into what I've learned works and doesn't work in strip clubs. If you want more expertise, check out my website, *www. stripper-book.com*; you'll see a list of seminars you can sign up for. It's a hands-on training you can receive by coming out with me and practicing your strategies and techniques on these girls, with me as your coach.

The Numbers Game

Stop worrying about your reputation. Girls jump from club to club often, and a new crop is always coming through. You don't have to change. Like with many things in life, it's always a numbers game. When it comes to sales, you need lots of activity to create a solid pipeline for future sales. It's the same with women. You have to spread it out when you're dating because you don't know who will pull through. Timing is key. It's not any different with strippers if you do these three things well: hit multiple strip clubs, network with multiple people in the club, and go out regularly. Your success rate will increase, and you will close deals!

Naturally, you will find tons of opportunities to take out strippers and pretty much do as much or as little as you want to do with them. These girls are less judgmental and more willing to accept your faults. They have many of their own drawbacks that they are insecure with, and this works in your favor. This is the opposite of regular bars in your town, where your reputation can get the best of you. Some decent girls you might actually want to introduce to Mom frequent there. Strip clubs are a completely different environment, and when it comes to your reputation, don't worry about it! You're not looking for your wife here. Never ever ever marry a stripper. My few buddies who have are miserable.

High Heels Story

I've pretty much always told the exotics what I do for a living. I'm in sales, and it's pretty obvious that I'm very friendly and outgoing. Once, I heard a buddy of mine tell a dancer that he was a race-car driver. I was puzzled at first at why he did this, because he drove a 1992 Nissan 200SX. That's far from a race car! The dancer was very intrigued and said, "That must be exciting and dangerous, going that fast." My buddy shrugged it off and replied, "Not really. It gets boring, going around in circles the whole time." His reply actually worked to his advantage because he didn't act all excited about it. It left her feeling like he was looking for something more exciting and possibly dangerous. She started thinking maybe he wanted her to be that outlet.

That observation had me thinking, *Why couldn't I act like somebody new at the strip club? These girls are all full of lies when they approach us. Why not us?* From the clear heels that make them six inches taller to their stage names that reference most automobiles, they are full of deceit. Even the costumes they have that symbolize Catwoman are a fantasy! It's all bullshit. That's when I decided to come up with the grandmother of all schemes to use in a strip club. I'll start off by telling you my old license plate had Vivid on it, and my friend bought me a T-shirt that said Vivid talent scout on the back.

I went to the strip club with three buddies, my cousin and two friends. It was my cousin's friend who owned the club, and we were invited in to check out the place. It was our first time there. The owner did not know what any of us did for a living, and I thought to myself, *why not make up a story to impress the dancers with?* We had an hour-long drive, so we came up with our new cool aliases in the car on the way there. When we got there, we had it all worked out, who was going to be whom. The owner greeted us and had a corner wraparound VIP booth ready when we got there. This definitely helped our cause.

When dancers came up to us, I did all the talking. I introduced myself as a talent scout for a division of Vivid Entertainment. I had instant credibility because of the T-shirt. I told one of the dancers that we were in town evaluating the girls tonight and that most porn stars started off as dancers first. The exotic started asking me about Steve Hirsch and contract girls of Vivid. Naturally she caught me off guard, and I said that I was from a new division called Gang Bang Enterprises. My replies were total bullshit, but it got me off the hook. I remembered Jenna Jameson started off as a Vivid girl, and a few other facts, but not much else!

I then introduced my two buddies as assistants like the key grip and lighting guy for our films. My cousin was an executive producer and I was main producer, and we were looking for scorching-hot talent. This is when it all started to come together. This girl went in the back and told the other strippers that we were there as scouts looking for new talent and to stop by our booth if they were interested in getting into porn. Oh my God, let me tell you how genius this was. We had stripper after stripper coming by, talking with us nonstop. I told the girls to keep it on the down low from management because we were acquaintances with the owner and didn't want to seem like we were cutting in on his girls. What this master approach made-up story did was allow us a ticket to hang out with the strippers outside the club.

One dancer tried to call my bluff and was skeptical. I said, "Let's go outside and look at my license plate." She grabbed a smoke, and I met her out front. I had a valet parking spot because I drove a nice SUV at the time. There it was, Vivid on the license plate! She had no doubts after that! She went in and bragged to her friends, and this was all at the beginning of the night. It was like we had a free pass to anything we wanted to know. They started telling us about sexual fantasies they had and what positions they preferred. The best part is, it got them horny! We had our pick of the litter, and naturally we had a hotel after party with a handful of them until the next morning. I'll leave the rest of the story up to your imagination and add it to my next book on memoirs of my life!

VII. Stripper Confessions

I wanted to add some important stories that the dancers told me, to help you understand why the mind of a stripper is so important. Plus it's pretty amazing what can happen to these girls from time to time, and it's flat-out funny what they get themselves into. In that previous story from the last section about making up who you want to be, the key there was having the confidence and details to pull it off. Being a good bullshitter helps, but you really have to have a great plan going in. From that night, I started realizing I could get tons of strippers to disclose private, secret information about themselves if they felt they could gain from telling it. That led to this final section about exotic dancer confessions.

Mary Jane

One girl told me how she loved to turn guys on. It didn't matter what you looked like or if you had money or not. What was important to her was that she could turn you on from start to finish. It got her off knowing you were excited by her. It came out in a conversation; she confessed to me of her getting gangbanged by several guys. One night, she was working, and a traveling college baseball team came into the club. She was attracted to a couple of the guys, and they invited her back to their hotel room after her shift and a few drinks. She was pretty daring and wanted to fuck these guys, so naturally she wasn't worried about getting raped, which is usually their number-one fear. She went up to their room and started making out with one of the players. The next thing you know, she told the roommate to join in. Then the coach stopped by, and she said he could watch and that she wanted him to jerk off on her.

These guys must've totally been thrown off by her forwardness. Like I said earlier, you have to be ready for her signs or advances, because once strippers make up their mind, you'd better follow through! They ended up gangbanging her. My getting her to think of these exciting times got her revved up for me! Not all girls are going to be like this, but many of these strippers will go through a period of time known as their "slut phase." This phase they go through will cause them to experiment with just about anyone and anything. From toys to threesomes, their excitement level is higher than ever before, so they need more to turn them on.

Mindy

I am friends with one stripper who is thirty-eight years old now and has been in the game for fifteen years. This woman has made a decent living at this profession and has had several surgeries throughout the years to keep up her appearance. One time I went over to her apartment. She had previously lived with her parents until she was about thirty and then purchased her first home in cash. Mindy had told me she felt unsafe at her previous house, so she sold it and instead liked to rent in this gated apartment complex. Crazy customers had followed her home before, and now that was eliminated by her new apartment. This is when I realized how important safety was to these girls who are lifers in the business.

We were hanging out and talking about crazy ex-boyfriends that she had in the past. One guy who stood out was an older gentleman in his sixties that she dated. She told me she liked hanging out with him because he wasn't too horny anymore and that he never had kids, so he liked her company and didn't mind spending the money for her time. He had very low self-confidence with beautiful women, and this way, by hanging out with her, it made him feel young and worthy. The part that stood out the most in this story was that when he had passed away, she got called by his attorney and invited to the reading of his will. The older gentleman had left her fifty-five thousand dollars in cash in a brown paper bag that he wanted to go to her tax-free. She asked me if I wanted to see it and then proceeded to pull a shoebox out of her closet. There it was, stacks of hundreds. I felt like I was in a scene from the movie *Blow*. It was beautiful! Better looking than her, in all reality.

The reason I'm telling you this story is that what I learned from her is that safety and sugar daddies are on these girls' minds. They need guys to pay their bills, and wills are just the bonus. Her biggest concern now was after that money ran out, how would she replace him for her income? It was like in sales, when you lose a big customer and now you're trying to figure out how to replace those dollars in your pay. This sucker paid her car payment and cell phone at least, with the money he spent on her each month. Who knows what else he paid for? Mindy took about a year off from the club and burned through all that money. Now she is back working again, trying to find new suckers to pay her bills, young or old!

Mercedes

Here is her Girls Gone Wild confession. I was friends with a gorgeous stripper who was my coach in her club. We used to go to Denny's for breakfast after her shift all the time, to discuss the night and her fucked-up mentality. One night after work, she and her girlfriend went to eat and ran into this group of outgoing guys at Denny's. Of course, both parties were outgoing, because they were both drunk at Denny's at three in the morning. Eventually, the guys invited them back to their hotel room and told them they were shooting a new Girls Gone Wild video that was coming out in six months. This particular stripper thought, *Why not?* This could be her shot at five minutes (or five seconds) of fame. That's why she decided to go to the hotel with these guys. She started off doing a masturbation scene for them and then stepped it up a notch and asked the cameraman to join. The cameraman then proceeded to shut the camera off and join her in the festivities. She told me she had so much fun and was so turned on by all this that she would definitely do it again. The funny part is, she never signed a waiver, and her footage was never seen in any video that I've watched.

My question to her was, "Are you sure they were really from Girls Gone Wild?" I don't think they carry badges around. Personally, I think these guys just had a camera and one hell of a bullshit story. But hey, who am I to bust up her story? It turned her on, and that's all that mattered. The point here is that girls love being naughty too. Obviously these guys appealed to her wild side. She admitted to me that she wanted a story that other dancers would admire. I'm not sure if it worked, but she did go to the club telling all the girls that she did a video for Girls Gone Wild and that in six months, it would be out. She received a lot of attention that week, and that, to her, was probably enough satisfaction.

Conclusion

The hard part is, after you have fun dating many strippers or doing God knows what, if you try to go back to conventional women, you might get bored easily. Be careful. You still want to be able to accept the normal, trustworthy girl. Also, the normal, vanilla-type girl needs to accept your past. This is an even harder concept to understand until you face it. I've been on a few dates where my date will go to the bathroom, and some girl will try to warn her at the sink about my past with strippers. Even other guys have hated on me and told the sweet girl I was seeing that I was a bad guy and I dated strippers all the time. Some of this was true, and some of it was a flat-out lie. Girls who listened to these jerks and wouldn't give me the time of day hurt my feelings. I guess I learned quickly that I didn't need them either if they were going to judge the book by its cover.

I have a thick skin and have never really cared what people have thought about me, as long as I treated people with respect. Character is what matters, not reputation. The sad part is that perception is reality, and no matter what you tell people, they will believe what they want to. I sleep well at night, and deep down, I tell the truth with these girls. I just go about it smoother and have a solid approach, but they always know the expectations and intentions I have with them.

If you're a guy who has a tender heart and worries about his reputation, then this lifestyle is probably not for you. I talked earlier about how these girls develop a perspective and a stripper mentality and view men a certain way in there. The same can happen to you. The deeper you go into the club to see what goes on, the more it changes your perspective on women. I guess the moral of the story is to just take it all in and realize every situation is different and don't put a lot of stock into anybody. Just have fun and enjoy the ride. It will turn out to be a life-changing experience for you if you take advantage of the information I've laid out for you. I hope you have learned more than you ever imagined about the life of a stripper and the strip-club scene. I look forward to answering any questions you may have or meeting you at one of my seminars and hands-on clinics. This is just the beginning of understanding how to have much more fun at the strip club, and we've only scratched the surface on giving you the knowledge of what I have spent the last ten years mastering. Thank you for purchasing this book, and please recommend it to several of your friends. I need all the support I can get and am very excited to write the sequel to this book.